THE LIFE AND SOLO PIANO WORKS OF THE UKRAINIAN COMPOSER MYROSLAV SKORYK

Victor Radoslav Markiw

With a Foreword by
Peter Kaminsky

The Edwin Mellen Press
Lewiston•Queenston•Lampeter

Library of Congress Cataloging-in-Publication Data

Markiw, Victor Radoslav.
The life and solo piano works of the Ukrainian composer Myroslav Skoryk / Victor Radoslav Markiw ; with a foreword by Peter Kaminsky.
p. cm.
Includes bibliographical references and index.
ISBN-13: 978-0-7734-3690-9
ISBN-10: 0-7734-3690-1
1. Skoryk, Myroslav Mykhailovych. 2. Skoryk, Myroslav Mykhailovych. Piano music. 3. Composers--Ukraine--Biography. I. Title.
ML410.S59855M37 2010
786.2092--dc22
[B]

2010007148

hors série.

A CIP catalog record for this book is available from the British Library.

Front cover photo: Composer portrait courtesy of Myroslav Skoryk

The Edwin Mellen Press
Box 450
Lewiston, New York
USA 14092-0450

The Edwin Mellen Press
Box 67
Queenston, Ontario
CANADA L0S 1L0

The Edwin Mellen Press, Ltd.
Lampeter, Ceredigion, Wales
UNITED KINGDOM SA48 8LT

Printed in the United States of America

The Life and Solo Piano Works of the Ukrainian Composer Myroslav Skoryk

To the Ukrainian Diaspora,
who have never forgotten
their homeland

Table of Contents

List of Examples

List of Figures

Foreword

In its frequency of occurrence, the theme of the "unjustly neglected artist" approaches the status of cliché and, consequently, becomes a tried and true subject for writers and scholars from all manner of disciplinary orientation. Certainly this unflattering categorization reflects my initial reaction to hearing the name Myroslav Skoryk and the claim for him as one of the most respected and original Ukrainian composers of the latter part of the twentieth century. In the process of coming to know his music, however, the "neglected artist" patina melted away in the wake of his inspiration, technical and compositional craftsmanship, and sheer élan.

As a composer, Skoryk invokes a dizzying array of styles and descriptive terms, including: Romantic lyricism; pedagogue and composer of music for children; nose-thumbing Bronx-cheering parodist; virtuoso writing; contrapuntist; pasticheur; Carpathian folk music; jazz and lounge idioms—sometimes all in the same piece! Take, for example, the second movement Waltz from *Partita No. 5*. The outer sections could be an alternate take from Ravel's *Valses nobles et sentimentales*: elegant, rich harmonies, well-proportioned phrases, characteristic rhythmic inflections, simple ternary form, etc. But the gnomish staccato trill heading into the middle section leads us down a rabbit hole to Chopinesque octave runs, jazz sequences with Lisztian overtones, a big glitzy show tune à la Andrew Lloyd Webber, a Debussy whole-tone riff, and a children's etude in repeated notes. Throughout Skoryk's piano music, the spirits of Bach (J.S. *and* P.D.Q.), Prokofiev, Puccini, Chick Corea, Debussy, Ravel, Count Basie, Satie, Liszt, Rachmaninoff, Beethoven, Chopin, and a host of others collide with each other in inventive and surprising combinations. Of course, such post-modern stylistic techniques as "polystylism" and "collage" come to mind, and yet inevitably fall short as over-simplistic and reductive. Within the wild panoply of his styles and genres lies a consistency of engagement and quality; more so, while its disparities are immediately evident, what might be termed the "logic of unpredictability" of Skoryk's music presents a much tougher nut to crack.

Talented author and pianist Victor Radoslav Markiw, whose diverse background makes him ideally suited to guide readers through the most important and representative of Skoryk's works, the music for solo piano, deftly handles the composer's complex artistic idiosyncrasy and even eccentricity. A concert pianist, educator, historian, and analyst, Professor Markiw possesses a depth of knowledge and understanding of Skoryk's piano music, arguably without equal, and certainly has created a Skoryk study unsurpassed amongst writings in English. Beginning with a biographical and stylistic overview, then focusing on a number of representative works demonstrating Skoryk's compositional progression over four decades from 1960 through the 1990s, and concluding with a close reading of the *Burlesque*, Professor Markiw presents a lucid and detailed exposition of the music. Besides its thorough scholarship and analysis, what sets Professor Markiw's work apart is the access he had to the composer and the subsequent transcriptions compiled through hours of personal interviews. Skoryk's thoughts on his music, when combined with Professor Markiw's biographical information, historical and stylistic insights, and expert analytical readings that consider both performance and scholarly perspectives, provide an unusually informative and fascinating view of the composer, accessible to non-specialists while at the same time providing valuable musical information to performers encountering this music for the first time. With the publication of this splendid study, Professor Markiw has taken an important step in securing Myroslav Skoryk's rightful place in the pantheon of contemporary composers.

Peter Kaminsky, Ph.D.
Associate Professor
University of Connecticut

Acknowledgments

I would like to express my gratitude and indebtedness to Professor Peter Kaminsky, whose ongoing guidance and support provided invaluable perspective as well as buttressing my decision-making during indecisive moments. I also would like to acknowledge and thank Dr. Neal Larrabee, Dr. Alain Frogley, Dr. Ronald Squibbs, Dr. Theodore Arm, and the late Peter Sacco. Of course, I extend a heart-felt thank you to Myroslav Skoryk, who kindly provided the necessary musical scores, was always available and eager to meet with me for one of our many interview sessions, and without whom this manuscript would not exist. A special thank you must go out to Dr. Richard Bass for his advice and encouragement and to Tracey Rudnick for introducing me to her highly productive research techniques. In addition, I would like to acknowledge my father, Bohdan Markiw, for his aid in translating sources, my sister Areta Heran and colleague Cecilia Mandrile for their assistance in preparing many score excerpts, and Oleksander Kuzyszyn of Duma Music for providing additional musical scores of Skoryk's works.

Finally, I must reserve a more personal thank you to all who offered support of another kind, that unique and priceless encouragement that comes only from family and friends. Without the input of these selfless individuals, I am not certain I would have made it through. Accordingly, I thank with fondness and warmth Ralf Carriuolo, Bernard Keilty, Maria Gogarten, Dan Shea, David Yeagley, Paul Ostrovsky, Katarina and David Rutkowski, Laurie and Phil Best, Maxim and Andrew Polonsky, Rosemary Noonan, Volodymyr Vynnytsky, and last, but certainly not least, my parents.

Chapter 1
An Overview of Skoryk's Life and Works

Introduction

This book provides the most extensive and comprehensive English language study to date of the internationally renowned Ukrainian composer Myroslav Skoryk. It includes a detailed discussion of his complete solo piano works written to date, most of which are quickly becoming available in music libraries across the globe. Available sources consulted for this research project include materials written in Ukrainian, Russian, and English. In addition, I conducted extensive interviews with Myroslav Skoryk during the month of December 2004.

Ukrainian literature on Skoryk is growing; however, in the English language, there are very few sources available. The existing biographies by O.S. Tymoshenko (2000), Yarema Yakubiak (1999), Liubov Kyianovska (1998) and Yuri Shchyrytsia (1979), provide different perspectives concerning Skoryk's life and music. While each of these sources presents a general outline of the composer's life and music, none concentrates solely on his solo piano works. My interviews with the composer have yielded much valuable information, including biographical and analytical material available only through access to the composer himself.

The purpose of this book is to make available to English-speaking readers an extensive introduction to Skoryk's solo piano music, including biographical information, compositional background, and structural analysis. I also hope this work will be of interest to pianists looking to familiarize themselves with Skoryk's piano music. In addition, this work may stimulate interest among

English-speaking scholars who have yet to explore the music of one of Ukraine's leading composers. Please note that my interviews with the composer occurred between December 10-13, 2004; all quotations attributed to the composer in this research project come from those interviews. A complete published list of Skoryk's piano works has been included in this book's Appendix in order to aid future research projects.

A Biographical Sketch

Myroslav Skoryk belongs in the forefront of well-known composers from Ukraine, which declared its independence in 1991. Although his name and music are known in many countries throughout the world, he continues underrated and deserving of appropriate recognition, a perspective, corroborated by Joseph McLellan, music critic for *The Washington Post*:

> To the best of my recollection, I never heard a note composed by Myroslav Skoryk until Wednesday night, when three of his pieces were played at the Chevy Chase Women's Club. He should be better known in this country; he is an original, a composer with a distinct identity, a mastery of many idioms—jazzy, folk-style and moderately avant-garde—that he uses to shape works embodying piquant contrast, convincing climaxes and sometimes impish wit (*The Washington Post*, (Washington), 26 February 2000, sec. C, p. 4).

Myroslav Skoryk was born on July 13, 1938, in western Ukraine's main city of Lviv, which at that time belonged to Poland. His parents were both educated in Austria at the University of Vienna and subsequently became educators. His father was a historian and ethnographer, while his mother was an accomplished chemist. Although his parents did not have special musical training, his mother played piano and his father played the violin. Young Myroslav was exposed to music in the household from an early age and took a particular liking to it.

Although his parents influenced Myroslav's early interest in music, no less important was the fact that in his family was a very famous diva of the twentieth century: "Myroslav Skoryk's great aunt was the famous Ukrainian soprano Solomea Krushelnitzka" (Stelmakh p. 12). Skoryk recalls: "I was strongly influenced by her remarkable musicianship and stage presence as well as the magical sounds of Puccini's operas." Among her artistic accomplishments was the second premiere of Giacomo Puccini's opera *Madame Butterfly* of 1904 in Brescia, Italy where she practically saved the opera after the first performance in Milan with another soprano; after Krushelnitzka's performance, the opera became world famous in the operatic literature. The ill-fated premiere and successful second performance are summarized by Matthew Boyden:

> Puccini withdrew the opera, returned his fee to the astonished La Scala, and set about revising his score, adding a tenor aria and cutting Act II into smaller units (the latter is sometimes labeled Act. III). Three months after the fiasco of La Scala, Puccini oversaw the second premiere in Brescia, with only one cast change [Solomea Krushelnitzka]. The new Madama Butterfly triumphed: Puccini was again Italian Opera's top dog (Boyden p. 371).

There were more premieres in Milan's La Scala, along with performances of Richard Strauss' *Salome* and *Elektra* under the baton of Arturo Toscanini with the composer present, who was enchanted by her performances. Ms. Krushelnitzka was also a beloved actress to musical audiences in Warsaw, especially her title role in Polish composer Stanislaw Moniuszko's *Halka*, and as a cast member in the company known as the Italian Opera, which made a world tour also featuring Enrique Caruso and Mattia Battistini.

The parents of young Skoryk recognized his talent and inclination towards music and consulted with Ms. Krushelnitzka on his future prospects as a musician. Upon determining that young Myroslav had extraordinary abilities as well as absolute pitch, she encouraged his entrance into the local music school. Skoryk states "It was Ms. Krushelnitzka who recommended serious musical study to my parents, enrolling me in the special music school for gifted children where I was admitted in 1945 as a piano student." The teachers and other students all recognized his talent in composing new songs and piano pieces, but his education would come to a sudden halt.

In 1947, Stalin's system of ethnic cleansing was reinstated in western Ukraine as well as in the other former Soviet republics. Stalin's regime focused on the Ukrainian people and their intelligentsia, many of whom were educated in foreign countries and possessed a broader outlook on the world and strong nationalistic feelings toward their own country. "This first assault on the Ukrainian intelligentsia preceded the general attack on the peasantry. Stalin clearly understood that the essence of Ukrainian nationhood was contained in the intelligentsia who articulated it" (Conquest p. 219).

During this time there were hundreds upon hundreds of railroad transports to Siberia where Ukrainians were loaded onto cattle cars and deported: "Thousands were shot, and many more sent to labor camps or deported—a figure of up to two million is usually given" (Conquest p. 334). A similar fate would also touch the Skoryk family. The eldest son was arrested first and most of the family, including Myroslav and his parents, were subsequently arrested. "We were deported to the small mining town of Antero-Sudchensk of Kemerova Oblast in western Siberia."

Skoryk's musical education was halted during this period but soon after arriving in Antero-Sudchensk, he was enrolled in the local music school where he majored in violin and piano. In fact, his music teachers were themselves victims of exile. His violin teacher was a musician from Lviv, who traveled to Siberia within the very same railroad cattle car that had held the young Skoryk. His piano teacher, as Skoryk recalls, was "a Muscovite, and had been a student of Sergei Rachmaninoff, and this was the cause of her punishment." This was the case because Rachmaninoff's decision to leave Russia during the 1917 revolution was viewed by the Soviet government as the act of a traitor, and any connection to the composer-pianist was considered grounds for punishment. In 1953, Stalin's death resulted in a thaw throughout the Soviet Union. Orest Subtelny writes:

> Stalin's death introduced a new era in Soviet history. Exhausting, wasteful, and irrational, the dictator's method of ruling by terror and duress could not be maintained indefinitely. Even the Soviet elite yearned for change . . . for the millions of Ukrainians incarcerated in the Siberian forced labor camps, de-Stalinization brought an unexpected reprieve: many of them were amnestied and allowed to return to their homes. (Subtelny p. 502)

As a result, in 1955, Skoryk and his family were permitted to return to Lviv which enabled the teenager to finish middle school and a seven-year course in music school focusing on the violin and piano. Skoryk immediately enrolled in the Lviv Conservatory's history and theory department and presented his piano works as an entrance exam.

At the conservatory, Skoryk received a solid foundation in composition and theory. Skoryk states "My teachers were well-known composers and educators, including Stanyslav Liudkevych (1879–1979), a graduate of the Vienna Conservatory, Roman Simovych (1901–1984), a graduate from the Prague Conservatory in 1933, and Adam Soltys (1890–1968), a graduate of the Berlin Conservatory." Skoryk's final exam piece was the Cantata *Vesna—Spring,* on verses of Ivan Franko (1856–1916) for soloists, mixed choir and symphonic orchestra. Skoryk also wrote some piano music during this time, including a cycle of piano pieces *V Karpatakh—In Carpathian Mountains* and the *Piano Sonata in C*, thus showing a predilection toward a genre that subsequently gave him recognition, and to some extent determined his creative direction.

In 1960, Skoryk enrolled in the postgraduate research program at the Moscow Conservatory where he studied with the celebrated composer Dmitri Kabelevsky. During this time, Skoryk composed music in a vast array of styles: symphonic, chamber, and vocal. Some works from this period include the *Suite in D Major for Strings*, *Sonata No. 1 for Violin and Piano*, and *Partita No. 1 for Strings* which soon became a popular piece. In addition, Skoryk also wrote several piano works such as the *Variations*, *Blues*, and *Burlesque*; the latter in particular gained much popularity and has been widely performed throughout concert halls around the world. His *Burlesque* came to be a required work in piano competitions, most notably the Vladimir Horowitz Piano Competition in Kiev, Ukraine, and also served as pedagogical material.

Skoryk graduated from the Moscow Conservatory in 1964 and took a teaching job at the Lviv Conservatory where he remained until 1966. Shortly thereafter, he accepted a position at the Kiev Conservatory where "Along with teaching composition classes, I also lectured in theory classes that focused on contemporary harmony techniques." The subject of Skoryk's dissertation, which he completed in 1964, was Prokofiev's music and is entitled *Osoblyvosti ladu muzyky S. Prokofieva; The Modal System of Prokofiev.* Skoryk also authored the book, *Struktura I vyrazhalna pryroda akordyky v muzitsi XX stolittia; (The Structural Aspects of Chords in Twentieth Century Music),* as well as numerous articles (see Appendix for information on these titles).

Works written during the 1970s consisted of some larger-scale compositions such as the *Violin Concerto No. 1*, *Partita No. 2 for Chamber Orchestra*, *Concerto for Orchestra—Carpathian* and the *Partita No. 3 for String Quartet*. Skoryk also became more active in writing for the piano. Dmitri Kabelevsky commissioned Skoryk to compose various pieces, including *Molodizhnyj Koncert—Concerto for The Young for Piano and Orchestra* and later his *Concerto No. 1 for Piano*, which was written specifically for the Dmitri Kabelevsky Competition for Young Pianists which is held in Kuibishev (today known as Samara), Russia. The concerto quickly became an obligatory work during the competition's third and final round. Skoryk also wrote many pieces for children, one of which bears the title *Z dytiachoho albomu* which translates to *From the Children's Album*. Two additional virtuosic works were written during this time: *Concerto No. 2 for Piano and Orchestra* and the *Concerto for Violoncello and Orchestra*, both of which have become standard concert repertoire in Ukraine. During the 1970s, Skoryk wrote two demanding piano pieces, *Partita No. 5* and *Toccata*, both of which have gained wide popularity.

Although Skoryk writes mainly in the genres of symphonic and chamber music, he has also written many pieces in the style of vaudeville and jazz, as well as music for films and the theater. The film *Tini zabutikh predkiv (Shadows of Forgotten Ancestors)* by Sergei Parajanov, for which Skoryk composed the musical score, was a winner of six International Film Festival awards. These pieces also impressed Dmitri Shostakovich, who wrote to Skoryk, enthusiastically praising his efforts after hearing them.

Along with his active career in composing, Myroslav Skoryk has devoted significant time to pedagogical and promotional activities. While teaching at the Kiev Conservatory (1966–1986), Skoryk taught an impressive list of composition graduates, including O. Balakauskas, Eugene Stankovych, Ivan Karabyts, Oleg Kyva, V. Zubytsky, Y. Vereshchagin, V. Shurneiko, V. Stepurko and O. Kozarenko. These composers have gone on to become well known in Eastern and Western Europe. In 1968, Skoryk became the Vice Chairman of the Ukrainian Composers Union, and Secretary of the Composers Union of the USSR. Skoryk's creative output as well as his pedagogical and public activities has made him a leading Ukrainian composer. In addition to his teaching post at the Kiev Conservatory, Skoryk became the chairman of the Composition Department at the Lviv Conservatory (1968) and instructed other talented composers including H. Havrylets, I. Nebesnyi, and B. Froliak.

During this same period (1966–1986), Myroslav Skoryk performed as a pianist and conductor in various tours throughout Ukraine, Russia, Latvia, Georgia, Poland, Germany, Canada, the United States, and Australia. These tours brought together various soloists, the Lviv Chamber Orchestra, and Skoryk, who was the artistic director in productions predominantly of his own music. In the late 1980s and early 1990s, Skoryk devoted his time to writing a set of six preludes and fugues. He states, "My [original] plan was to write a cycle of twelve preludes and fugues in chromatic succession in major modes and in which serial and dodecaphonic techniques dominate." However, this plan changed as Skoryk wrote his preludes and fugues in a style he labels "neo-modern." Currently, this cycle remains a work in progress and contains only six preludes and fugues ranging in major keys from C to F.

Another interesting piano work of the early 1990s is the *Paraphrase on themes from Giacomo Puccini's opera Madame Butterfly*, in which Skoryk reveals, "I had in mind composing this piece as homage to commemorate my great aunt Solomea Krushelnitzky, who was unsurpassed in Puccini's *Butterfly* role." Skoryk also says, "interestingly enough, the themes from this opera have not been utilized as piano paraphrased selections, as was done with operas by Verdi or works by composers like Paganini. So in this respect, I was eager to write a large and technically demanding piece."

Skoryk was also involved in many other compositional projects during the 1990s. His *Concerto No. 2 for Violin and Orchestra* received critical acclaim in Ukraine, along with his *Concerto No. 3 for Piano and Orchestra* (a version for String Quartet, Double Bass, and Drum exists), *Partita No. 6 for Strings*, *Partita No. 7 for Wind Quintet*, and the *Sonata No. 2 for Violin and Piano*. The late 1990s yielded a monumental opera, *Moses*. Skoryk states, "The basis for this opera was the same titled poem written by the Ukrainian classic poet Ivan Franko." *Moses* was "an unexpected step out of his [Skoryk's] usual compositional style [and it] exemplifies the composer's first attempt in this genre" (Stelmakh p. 15). *Moses* premiered in the Opera Theatre of Lviv with such success that it was produced in the Ukrainian capital Kiev as well as in Ivano-Frankivsk and the Polish cities of Warsaw and Posen. Another surprise was when "Pope John Paul II attended one of the first rehearsals of Skoryk's opera, *Moses*" (Stelmakh p.15).

During this later period of the 1990s, Skoryk wrote the cantata, *Hamaliia for soloists, mixed chorus and orchestra* with text by the Ukrainian poet Taras Shevchenko (1814–1861). Skoryk says, "The work *Hamaliia* is a spiritual concerto requiem on canonical texts for soloists and mixed a cappella chorus." Since 2001, Skoryk has been busy writing for the violin, a fruitful time that has yielded his *Violin Concertos Nos. 3, 4* and *5*. For the past several years the composer has been living between the two Ukrainian cities of Lviv and Kiev. He is a professor and dean at the Department of History of Ukrainian Music, and Chairman of the Ukrainian Center of Music at the P. I. Tchaikovsky National

Academy of Ukraine in Kiev. Other posts held by Skoryk include a professorship and dean of composition at the Mykola Lysenko Music Academy in Lviv.

The focus of this book is on Skoryk's piano works, with specific emphasis on his compositions for piano solo. The study of these pieces provides insight into the compositional and interpretative style that has made Skoryk a significant contemporary composer. The following is a complete list of his piano works to date:

1. *Prelude and Nocturne*—1955
2. Cycle of pieces: *In the Carpathians*—1959
3. *Sonata in C*—1959
4. *Variations for piano*—1962
5. *Burlesque*—1963
6. *Blues*—1963
7. Cycle of pieces: *From the Children's Album*—1966
8. *Partita No. 5*—1975
9. *Toccata*—1978
10. *Six Preludes and Fugues*—1989
11. *Paraphrase on opera themes of Giacomo Puccini's Madame Butterfly*—1992
12. *Six Jazz Pieces*—1993
13. *Melody*—1994

Stylistic Development

The second half of the twentieth century, the time frame for Skoryk's creations, was a period in which composers sought to find their own style by experimenting with a variety of musical possibilities. It was not easy for Skoryk to find his own voice with such a multitude of tendencies. Regarding the multiple influences in his music, Skoryk describes it as "a classic style that germinates from Prokofiev, Bartók, Szymanowski, and Shostakovich." Moreover, his style is further based on the foundation of tonal principles of music from the past, however, not excluding occasional references to dodecaphonic and serial music – in spite of his general attitude toward these techniques (see below). Here we can put all possible styles such as neoclassicism, which Skoryk states "comes from Stravinsky," minimalism, electronic music, and jazz elements, for which Skoryk expresses a special affinity toward the musical works of George Gershwin, Aaron

Copland and Leonard Bernstein. It is hard to pinpoint whether there is a principal trend during this epoch period. Skoryk elaborates on this idea: "Every composer of today strives to find his or her own stylistic foundation in order to realize a personal identity and to form a unique style."

During his creative life, Myroslav Skoryk has adopted a variety of features and familiarized himself with many different composers. But one style remained outside his creative path. He is fundamentally opposed to atonal and serial music pioneered by Arnold Schoenberg and says, "I reaffirm these views in my musical and theoretical essays." He believes that atonality does not increase a composer's possibilities but rather diminishes them, which in turn creates a programmed and schematic output violating creative freedom. This, he further states, "stifles the composer's intuition and makes those works uniform, monotonous, and rather uninteresting." Mr. Skoryk deals with this topic in an article titled "Prokofiev and Schoenberg" which he wrote and had published in the journal *Sovetskaya Muzyka* (*Soviet Music*), No. 1, in 1962. Boris Schwarz relates in his book a discussion he had with Skoryk regarding this topic:

> Skoryk's attitude can be summarized in four words: innovation—yes, avant-garde—no. He admits that certain modern techniques—new sonorities and aleatory effects or the method of *collage*—can be found in works in young Soviet composers. He is not in favor of these techniques and also rejects dodecaphony, which is by now a dead issue. . . . Skoryk shows his ignorance by asserting that Schoenberg and Webern "deny the previous musical experience." This misconception is widespread among Soviet composers, who parrot old and outworn slogans. . . . Skoryk is typical of a young breed of Soviet composers who are torn between enlightenment and conventionality (Schwarz p. 509).

It is interesting to note that Skoryk's current views (Schwarz's interviews with Skoryk date back to the 1960s) on these issues have not changed as related to me in more recent interviews (2004) I conducted with him. In general, the music most influential on Skoryk's style is largely tonal, while still incorporating twentieth-century trends. Nonetheless, Skoryk has interesting thoughts about the relative value of atonal music, which he states "is constructed not on the new findings of musical expression, but on the negation of tonal music, which is subordinate and relative." Skoryk goes on to say:

> It did not happen, as Schoenberg stated, that his invention of dodecaphony provided the security for a domination of German music for many years. In contrast, this technique didn't become dominant and music constructed on these principles occupies a small part in the history of music as well as in the life of contemporary music.

When describing the influences and creative path of his own works, Skoryk adds:

> The major influence on much of my music comes from the following composers: Ravel, Debussy, and Prokofiev. In the music of these composers we see traditional "old tonal music" with brilliant findings in modal structures and new harmonic revelations. This, in turn, made their music "classical" although mostly written in the 20th century. In the first place, it refers to the folkloric basis contained in many works of these composers, as well as neo-classical tendencies in later works of Igor Stravinsky. Furthermore, the great influence of Expressionism in Alban Berg's opera *Wozzek* shows Berg maintaining a mixture of tonal structure with dodecaphonic elements. There is a suitable balance of all musical styles during the time Berg wrote this opera.

Another layer of Skoryk's music reveals the influence and use of jazz elements. Skoryk notes that in the former Soviet Union jazz "was forbidden until 1956 when the ruling party lifted this ban, at first with certain reluctance; soon after, however, jazz music made an enormous impression on the country's musicians." Frederick Starr writes, "Amid the general reaction against the extreme regimentation of the Stalin years in 1955 and 1956, the government's anti-jazz persecution eased up. Literally hundreds of small combos were formed in institutes and universities across the USSR. Few of the musicians could actually play jazz, but most affected what they thought to be the mannerisms of true jazzmen, pouring out their feelings to rapt audiences in search of candor and authenticity" (Starr p. 245). In searching for his own style, the influence of jazz created a strong basis for Skoryk's music. Skoryk notes, "The influence of

Debussy's impressionism as well as Stravinsky's fauvism in my piano cycle *In Carpathian Mountains*, along with the influence of Prokofiev's style in my *Suite in D for Strings* and Alban Berg's in the *Sonata in C*, is evident." At the same time, Skoryk's music clearly developed traditions of Ukrainian composers such as Mykola Lysenko, Stanislav Liudkevych, Lev Revutsky, and Boris Lyatoshynsky. Skoryk's Cantata *Vesna—Spring* (written as a graduation project) as well as his work throughout the 1970s manifests a polishing of his own style based on a synthesis of the elements previously mentioned.

Throughout this process of development, Skoryk assimilates a multitude of artistic currents and is successful in crystallizing his trademarks; indeed their manifestations become so clear that one can recognize his different stylistic tendencies by ear. Here, I provide a brief summary of Skoryk's stylistic developments, chronologically listed and as they appear in Liubov Kyianovska's book *Myroslav Skoryk: Creative Portrait of the Composer in a Mirror of Time*. Skoryk approved of this stylistic breakdown of his music as expressed to me in our interviews.

On the Brink of Maturity (1955–1964)

This first period consists of the piano cycle *V Karpatakh—In the Carpathians* with its use of folkloric elements from the music of Ukrainians (Hutsuls) living in the Carpathian Mountain region. The Cantata *Vesna—Spring*, which is based on a tradition of classic Ukrainian composers, including Mykola Lysenko, Stanislav Liudkevych, and Lev Revutsky, along with the *Suite for Strings,* contains what Skoryk says is, "a strong similarity to Prokofiev's style." In spite of the influences of other composers in all these works, Skoryk's personality and individual style are apparent and evolve from a synthesis of folk aspects and contemporary possibilities of expression associated with jazz rhythms and inflections. In addition, the *Sonata No. 1 for Violin and Piano* and the *Burlesque* for solo piano are works that have entered the mainstream concert repertoire and are widely used as pedagogical material in Ukraine and abroad. The significant solo piano works written during this period are as follows:

Prelude & Nocturne (1955)
Cycle—*In the Carpathians* (1959)
Piano Sonata in C (1959)
Piano Variations (1962)
Burlesque (1963)
Blues (1963)

The Wave of New Folklore (1965–1972)

This period titled by the musicologist Liubov Kyianovska references the tendency of select Ukrainian composers who turned to folklore sources (many of which come from antiquity) and gave these songs a modern interpretation. In Ukraine, the composers Leonid Hrabovsky, Lesia Dychko, Eugen Stankovych, Ivan Karabyts and others, represented this genre. Skoryk, however, had begun to work in this manner earlier and was improving and perfecting this wave of folkloric composition. Skoryk refers to this "new folkloristic wave" as "representing the contemporary absorption and rethinking of the folk song." Boris Schwarz elaborates on Skoryk's view:

> There are new principles of quotation, new realizations of folkish or stylized idioms through new procedures of modal harmonization, colouristic sounds, and formal shapes. There emerge more complex relationships between compositional concepts and folklore: the discovery of hidden modal and structural phenomena of folk melos, and especially the discovery of the musical practices of folk musicians who achieve interesting effects through intentional digressions from the tempered scale (Schwarz p. 509).

The most important works of Skoryk during this period include the *Hutsulskyi Tryptykh—Hutsul Triptych* for symphony orchestra, inspired by and used in Sergei Parajanov's film *Shadows of Forgotten Ancestors*, as well as *Recitatives and Rondo* for violin, violoncello and piano, and the cycle of piano pieces *From the Children's Album*. Especially successful during this period was the *Concerto No. 1 for Violin and Orchestra* and the *Concerto for Orchestra—*

Carpathian, both of which were received with acclaim by critics and audiences throughout the world. Only one solo piano work was completed during this period: *From the Children's Album* (1966).

Forward to Classical Perfection and on the Edge of Neoclassicism (1973–1978)

In this period, Skoryk begins to step away from folk influences and aim toward classical perfection. This does not mean that he abandons folkloric writing altogether, but that these elements became more or less subsidiary. This period includes the following works: *Partita No. 2 for Chamber Orchestra*, *Partita No. 3 for String Quartet*, and the popular *Toccata* for piano solo. Interestingly enough, within this period Skoryk composes his *Partita No. 5* for piano, where he explores a new method of composition not seen previously in his works. This so-called "new method" evident in the *Partita No. 5* is termed by Skoryk "stylistic game." Its heading, *In Modo Retro—In Old Style,* hints at what follows: a conglomeration of various stylistic hints and genres of composers like Bach, Ravel, Chopin, Liszt, Schumann and Rachmaninoff. This style brings to mind the *polystylistic* composition of which Alfred Schnittke has most recently become the most well-known exponent. Piano solo works written during this period are:

Partita No. 5 (1975)
Toccata (1978)

Signs of Neo-Romanticism (1982–1983)

To this period belong the *Concerto No. 2 for Piano and Orchestra* and the *Concerto for Violoncello and Orchestra.* This period was the beginning of Skoryk's predilection for this genre. Note that the soloist, whose writing up to this point was predominantly virtuosic in nature, is now focused on the inner feelings so as to carry a "message" with the intent of transmitting this to the audience. These two concertos have a neo-romantic inclination, often transgressing into high-voltage expressionism. Furthermore, these works demonstrate a break in the evolution of Skoryk's music that previously was less reliant on neo-romantic tendencies. When discussing his thoughts about this period, Skoryk comments, "A common trend can be observed in Western music, which, at this time, turned to older, previous sources of musical expression." Skoryk did not compose any solo piano music during this short period.

In the Labyrinths of Stylish Games (1984–1999)

Works written in this period belong to the category of "neo-modernism" according to Kyianovska. The often unexpected stylistic intertwining of different periods and genres as well as diverse themes and pitch collections are explored. This trend begins with an earlier work, Skoryk's *Partita No. 5* for piano, and continues with his piano cycle *Six Preludes and Fugues*. A similar style is evinced by the *Sonata No. 2* for violin and piano, the *Diptych for Strings*, A-RI-A for violoncello and piano, *Partita No. 3* for string quartet, *Partita No. 7* for wind quintet, and the *Concerto No. 3* for piano, strings and bass drum. Regardless of the multi-stylistic methods contained in these works, the composer's individuality is clearly felt. Piano solo works written during this period include:

Six Preludes and Fugues (1986–89)
Paraphrase on opera themes of Giacomo Puccini's "Madame Butterfly" (1992)
Six Jazz Pieces (1993)
Melody (1994)

Most Recent Work (1999–2004)

Works of this period show Skoryk once again changing his compositional path. He practically avoids altogether the inclination toward neo-modernism and polystylism and produces works, as he explains, "constructed in a more pure style in which the harmonic language or intonational findings are consistent throughout." referencing his monumental opera *Moses* and *Spiritual Concert-Requiem*, as well as the *Cantata*: *Hamaliia*. The quintessential works of these last years are his *Violin Concertos with Orchestra No. 3, 4,* and *5*, written respectively in 2002, 2003, and 2004. As Skoryk's creative life continues it would be reasonable to expect additional new works in this field from him. His current compositional projects include *Piano Concerto No. 4* which he has been trying to fit into his busy teaching and performance schedules.

Chapter 2

The Solo Piano Works In Analysis

In spite of the fact that Myroslav Skoryk's works gravitate toward the symphonic and chamber-instrumental genre, his piano music also represents a significant part of his oeuvre which includes three concertos for piano and orchestra, together with the above-mentioned works for solo piano. What follows is a brief analysis of Skoryk's early piano works written while still a student.

In Skoryk's music, several characteristic scales and modes are used, including modes that originate from the Ukrainian Carpathian region. The list below provides an introduction to specific modes and scales that will be referred to during the overview of the piano works. Modes that are native to the Carpathian region were collected and studied by Skoryk, who, like Bartók, spent a considerable amount of time researching indigenous music.

1. **Whole Tone Scale**:

2. **Mixolydian Mode.** Equivalent to a major scale with lowered 7th:

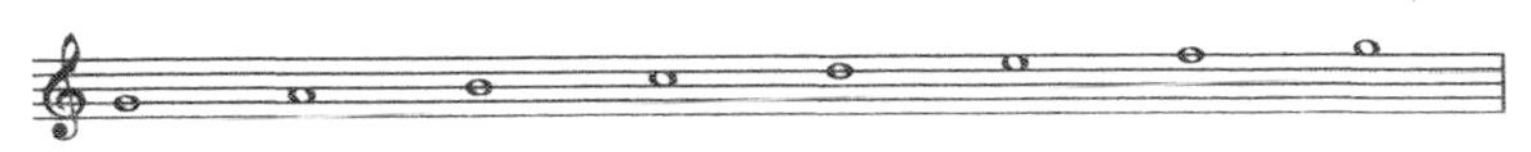

3. **#4, #6 Carpathian Mode (Hutsul Mode).** The lower tetrachord is identical to that of the Hungarian minor scale, the upper to that of the Dorian mode:

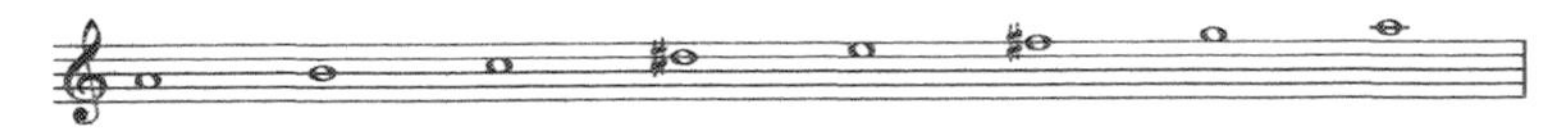

4. **Hungarian minor scale.** (Augmented 2nd between scale degrees 3-4, and 6-7):

5. **Flatted 2nd Mode.** The flatted 2nd scale degree mode, which shares similarities to the Phrygian Mode and natural minor scale:

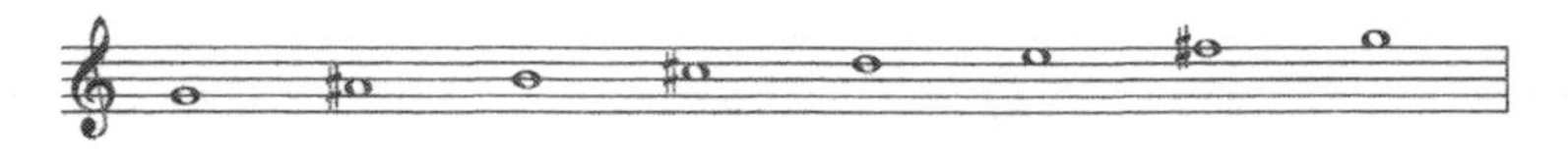

6. **#2, #4 Mode**. (Augmented 2nd between scale degree 1-2 and #4):

7. **Huculian Mode**. Also indigenous to the "Hutsuls" (from Ukraine's Carpathian region), this mode's first five notes are identical to the octatonic scale's whole step/half step pattern:

8. **Octatonic Scale:**

One aspect of Skoryk's harmonic language may be summarized as the juxtaposition of tonal and atonal practice. This is achieved by his selective use of set classes intertwined with more standard tonal principles. An example of this is Skoryk's *Burlesque*, the topic of discussion in Chapter 3. Another important harmonic feature is Skoryk's use of jazz harmony and style in a great number of works in addition to a distinct and recurring signature compositional trait described here as "semitonal interval game." The interval of a semitone is a dominating hallmark of Skoryk's compositions and often occurs as a tritone substitution to the dominant. Perhaps the semitone finds its lineage in Skoryk's predecessors, the previously mentioned Lviv School of composers. When discussing this western Ukrainian school of composers Andrey Olkhovsky writes:

> What attracts attention in their means of expression is their broad and free treatment of folk music material which they employ as a thematic basis, their extensive application of the variation principle of development and elaboration, the complexities of their harmony, their frequent use of semitone intervals, and in general their tendency towards complex harmonic timbres and freedom of linear exposition and textural development (Olkhovsky p. 251).

Olkhovsky's summation of Ukrainian composers and their use of indigenous folk music (particularly "Hutsul" folk music) clearly foreshadows Skoryk's similar utilization. Olkhovsky continues:

> A noteworthy characteristic of the creative work of the Lviv composers is their extensive use of local folk music . . . the use of such local musical dialects had played an important role in the works of such prominent reformers of contemporary music as Béla Bartók. In the present context it is a matter of the "Hutsul" idiom, which has acquired a definite individuality and significance. Its employment and development by composers would contribute significantly to the development of the national originality of Ukrainian music (Olkhovsky p. 259).

Skoryk's integration of the above-mentioned styles gives rise to an eclectic musical mix within a unique and personal style. Robert Morgan's summary of Bartók's style also applies to Skoryk's, especially when he states ". . . the eclecticism of Bartók's own mature compositional style, which draws upon many different, even seemingly opposed, sources yet synthesizes them within a completely consistent and personal idiom" (Morgan p. 109).

Generally, Skoryk's rhythmic practice features standard time signatures and rhythmic note values but relies heavily on syncopation, which is an inherent attribute of both jazz and Ukrainian Carpathian folk music. Skoryk's use of form adheres to conventional formal designs (and hybrids thereof) such as binary, ternary, sonata, rondo, and sonata-rondo with a generally symmetrical grouping of phrases.

Student Works—General Analysis

***Prelude & Nocturne* (1955)**

This is the first piece that Skoryk has permitted me to discuss in relation to his piano compositional output. Although it is not his first piano composition, he considers this *Prelude & Nocturne* to be the beginning and source of his compositions for piano solo. This is undoubtedly the work of a novice composer as Skoryk states: "This piece was written under the evident spell of Beethoven's piano music. This is most evident in the theme, which is very short, its development, modulatory sequences and clearly Beethovenian classic harmony."

In this derivative work one can find some interesting features: for example, the use of the interval of the melodic augmented 2nd (#7—b6) in mm. 3 and 4, what Skoryk says is "characteristic of Ukrainian folk music."

Example 2.1, Myroslav Skoryk, *Prelude*, mm. 1-5

Skoryk also transposes the main theme a major second lower (D-minor to C-minor) during the second exposition (m.11) that Skoryk links to "peculiarities of Slavic modes." No less original is the Prelude's ending, mm. 56-59. These final bars contain a "final recitative solo" which anticipates the recitative style of the composer in his later works.

Example 2.2, Myroslav Skoryk, *Prelude*, mm. 6-15

Example 2.3, Myroslav Skoryk, *Prelude*, mm. 56-59

The *Nocturne* (in C) is clearly based on Chopin's *Nocturnes* and shows Skoryk's technical fluency in classical methods, broad melodies, logical harmonic progressions and the use of the flatted second degree (Neapolitan Sixth, m. 22). These elements take place within a conventional phrase organization. The sentence structure 2 + 2 + 4 (mm. 1-8) is repeated in mm. 9-16 completing the broader 8 + 8 phrase structure. A development of the opening material in two-bar segments begins in m. 17, showing Skoryk's adherence to traditional techniques (see Example 2.4).

Example 2.4, Myroslav Skoryk, *Nocturne*, mm. 1-23

Cycle *In the Carpathians* (1959)

These four piano pieces are full of Ukrainian folk melodies from the Carpathian Mountains:

1. Boiko Song
2. In the Forest
3. Singing in the Mountains
4. Kolomyika

The titles of these pieces can be explained as follows. *Boiko Song* (Pisnia boika) derives from the ethnic group of Ukrainians—the Boikos—who have what Skoryk calls "peculiar folklore." In this piece Skoryk uses a folk song derived from this region for his main theme. The second and third pieces *In the Forest* (U lisi) and *Singing in the Mountains* (Spiv u horakh) are evocations of their respective titles and the fourth is *Kolomyika*—the name for a specific circle dance in duple meter, which derives from the name of the mountain town Kolomya in Ukrainian Carpathia.

Although Skoryk wrote *In the Carpathians* during his student years, this work contains some musical details which evidence independent thinking and point toward the future style of the composer. This is less evident in both the *Boiko Song* and *Singing in the Mountains,* because as Skoryk says, "I harmonize these folk songs in an impressionistic language and disperse them throughout the entire keyboard in a quasi Liszt-Rachmaninoff texture." Notwithstanding the complexities in these harmonizations, the use of Carpathian folklore coloring makes these pieces especially attractive. The simple lyrical themes from *Boiko Song* (in the Lydian Mode) and *Singing in the Mountains* (with the melodic span of the fifth) are harmonized with complex chords, which, according to Skoryk, "should imitate the murmur of trees, and the blowing of wind thereby mimicking a mountain atmosphere." During my meeting with Skoryk, the composer emphasized these melodies by notating the original folk themes shown below in Example 2.5:

Example 2.5, Boiko Song theme, mm. 6-10

And this is the folk theme *Singing in the Mountains*:

Example 2.6, *Singing in the Mountains theme*, mm. 18-21

Especially interesting are the intricate sliding chromatic chords in the middle section of *Singing in the Mountains* mm. 18-21. The composer's creative ability shows itself in how he manages to harmonize the melodic line. Measures 18-21 contain the same melodic note, but harmonized with different chords. (Note: reduction supplied by Skoryk)

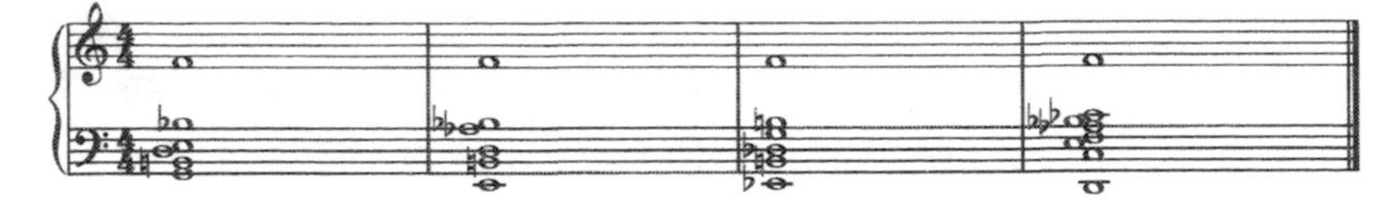

Example 2.7, *Singing in the Mountains* reduction of theme, mm. 18-21

And here are measures 18-21, as they appear in the piano score.

Example 2.8, Myroslav Skoryk, *Singing in the Mountains*, mm. 18-21

Skoryk also employs the technique of canonic imitation beginning at m. 32 (see Example 2.9).

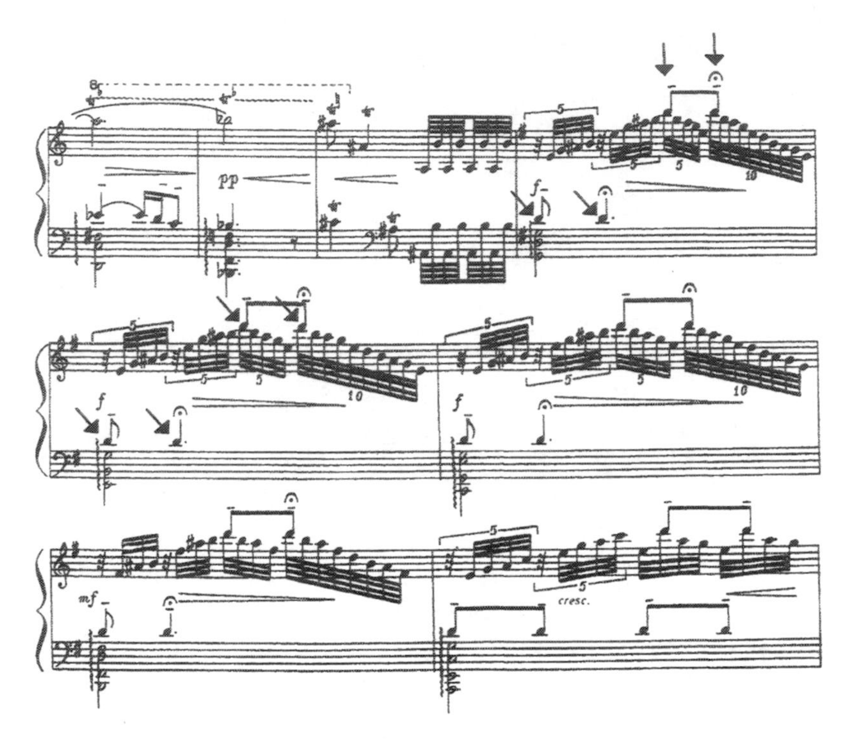

Example 2.9, Myroslav Skoryk, *Singing in the Mountains*, mm. 29-36

The second piece *In the Forest* demonstrates for the first time Skoryk's skill in working with dance idioms of the *Kolomyika* and fitting them into a non-traditional harmonic context. The influence of Bartók's music is obvious in that Skoryk uses the set class (0167) in mm. 1-2, also commonly known as the "Bartók" tetrachord. This tetrachord containing the pitch classes D-Eb-G#-A inflects the opening melody in D major. The Eb and G# (b2, #4) provide modal coloring, a variant of the previously mentioned modes. Interesting techniques in this ternary miniature include a gradual crystallization of dance themes from the introduction in which a "cuckoo" sound is imitated in the melody by sixteenth to dotted-eighth note rhythms in m. 5.

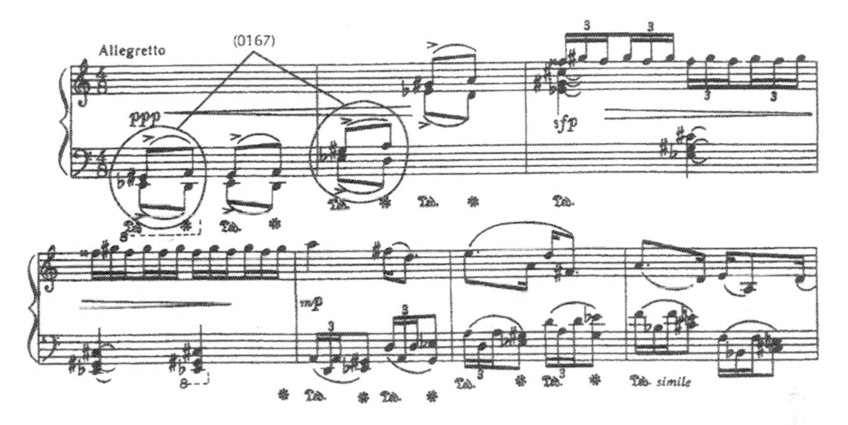

Example 2.10, Myroslav Skoryk, *In the Forest*, mm. 1-7

This is followed in m. 13 by an elaborated dissonant setting of the dance theme, the melody in pentatonic mode and transformed into what Skoryk referred to as "highly syncopated jazz rhythms."

Example 2.11, Myroslav Skoryk, *In the Forest*, mm. 13-15

Regarding the combining of Ukrainian folk elements and jazz, the musicologist Liubov Kyianovska writes "The first attempt to find a common denominator among two distant folklore cultures becomes a characteristic feature of Skoryk's works and in particular, his late works" (Kyianovska p. 41) (see Example 2.12).

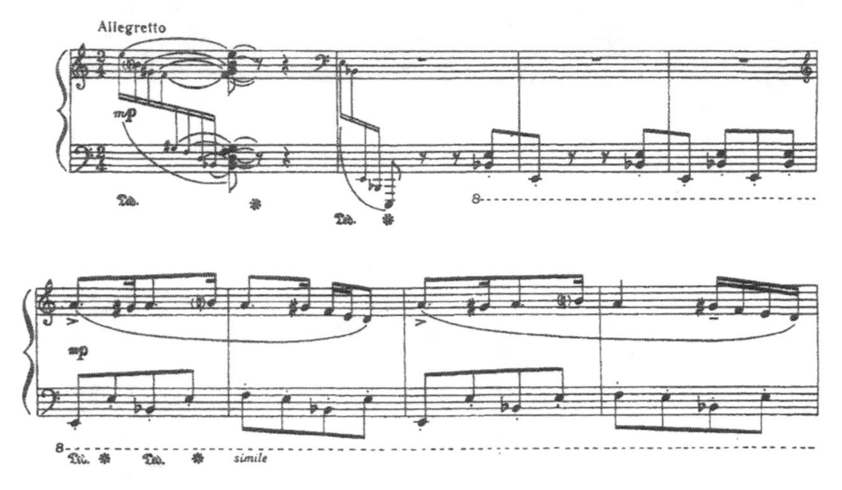

Example 2.12, Myroslav Skoryk, *Kolomyika*, mm. 1-8

The *Kolomyika* has become the most popular piece from this cycle. After four measures of introduction, where the rhythmic accompaniment is formed on the pitches E, B-flat, we hear an eight-measure folk theme in the Hutsul Mode, a D minor scale containing a raised fourth scale degree (see p. 17 no. 3).

The next eight-measure phrase (mm. 13-20), based on an ostinato figure in the accompaniment with its varied rhythm and octave displacement, contains what Skoryk calls "a whimsical and unstable theme embellished with figurations and melismatics characteristic of violin playing of country musicians" (see Example 2.13).

Example 2.13, Myroslav Skoryk, *Kolomyika*, mm. 13-20

A new theme appears in A minor in m. 21 and replicates a masculine male dance with characteristic stamping. This new section imitates the village musician and the stamping dance is executed by dissonant arpeggiated chords descending chromatically: A-E-G-sharp, G-sharp-D-sharp—G, etc.

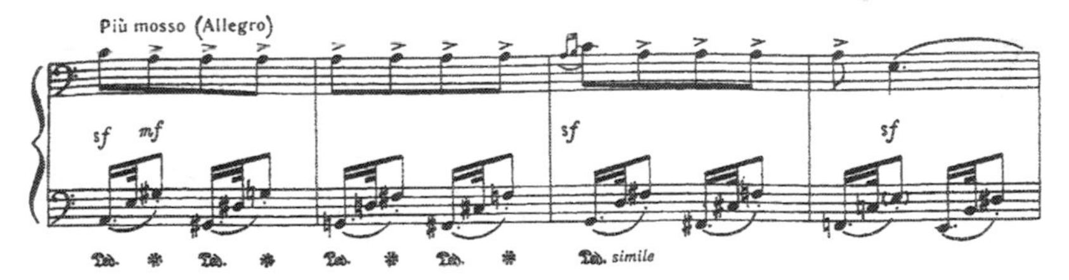

Example 2.14, Myroslav Skoryk, *Kolomyika*, mm. 21-24

The middle section beginning at m. 49 is totally opposite in the sense that there is no trace of the *Kolomyika*, but instead the "coloristic image of a landscape" as Skoryk says, "and [it] is intended to evoke the Carpathian flute—Sopilka (in pentatonic mode) and gives the feeling as if it were played in the mountains with a background drone similar to a village double bass."

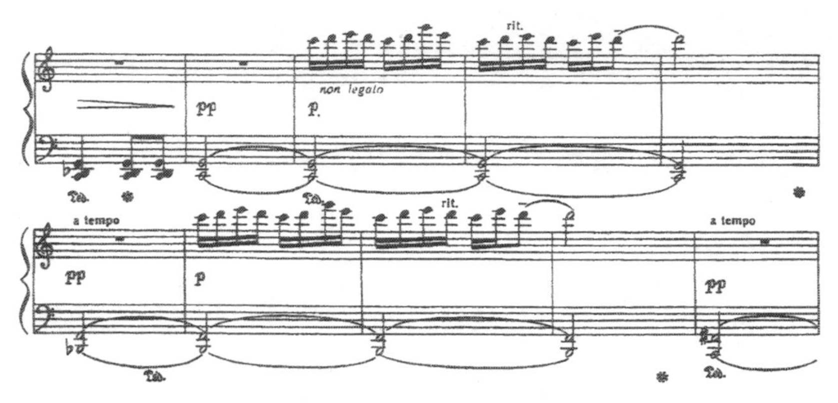

Example 2.15, Myroslav Skoryk, *Kolomyika*, mm. 50-59

This composition reveals Skoryk's new and original approach to the popular Carpathian dance, which became what the composer claims, was "a new stylistic development in Ukrainian music of the time."

***Sonata in C* (1959)**

Consisting of one movement, the *Sonata in C* was composed during Skoryk's studies in the conservatory (1958-59), which initiated a new direction in his compositions. One of the main features of this period was a tendency towards expressive romanticism, which would later appear in his *Symphonic Poem* titled *Waltz* along with his *Concerto No. 2 for Piano and Orchestra* and the *Concerto for Violoncello and Orchestra.* It is interesting to note that these works are almost entirely lacking in folk elements.

In this work, Skoryk experiments with combinations of major and minor intervals of the second. Skoryk notes: "My intention is based on experiments of minor and major seconds, not related to ordinary chromatics, but a progression of different diatonic successions used to fill a comparably wider interval." In a general sense this becomes one of the composer's hallmarks and represents a significant structural feature of many of his works. This influence clearly comes from Bartók's similar procedure in his music, about which Bryan Simms writes:

"Bartók described a type of melody that he had begun to use twenty years earlier, in which the initial pitches chromatically fill a small boundary interval. He attributed this type of chromaticism to the conflation of several diatonic modes" (Simms p. 215). Skoryk, during one of our meetings, notated the following examples beginning with his theme from the *Sonata in C*, which show the developing chromaticism in his main thematic material in later works.

Example 2.16, Myroslav Skoryk, *Sonata in C*, main theme in his early *Sonata in C*

Example 2.17, Myroslav Skoryk, *Symphonic Poem-Waltz*, bass ostinato

Example 2.18, Myroslav Skoryk, *Concerto for Violoncello*, leitmotiv

Example 2.19, Myroslav Skoryk, Ostinato from the Finale of the *Piano Concerto No. 3* (transposed and supplied by the composer)

In this manner the composer's style was crystallizing beginning with his student work, the *Sonata in C*. In this sonata Skoryk turns to complex six-note chords, which he uses, for the second part of the opening main theme figure in m. 2. The combination of the first melodic element and the following harmonic element, which together form the opening theme, provides the principal material for the entire sonata.

Example 2.20, Myroslav Skoryk, *Sonata in C*, mm. 1- 4

During one of our discussions regarding the value of this sonata, Mr. Skoryk told me that this is not a fully mature work: "This sonata's construction is rather primitive because its main leitmotiv element repeats itself too often and saturates the texture of the piece. Another fault is the expressive over-exaltation lacking naturalness, along with a hint of far-fetched artificiality." At the same time, however, Skoryk states that the *Sonata in C* "was to become a primary source for later works as well as the aesthetic direction for the compositions that fit within my expressive romantic style." Notwithstanding its student-like conventionality in regard to form and thematic development, the *Sonata in C* proves an important exercise and catalyst for more mature works to follow.

Variations for Piano (1962)

Skoryk states "*Variations for Piano* is a work of simple student management." This is understandable because it was written under the tutelage of Dmitri Kabelevsky in his class at the Moscow Conservatory where Skoryk was a research student. Skoryk was following his teacher's wishes and admitted to me the influence coming from both Kabelevsky and Sergei Prokofiev, who held Kabelevsky in high esteem. One possible model on which Skoryk bases his variations is the second movement of the 3rd Piano Concerto by Sergei Prokofiev. Concerning the influence of Prokofiev's concerto, Skoryk further states, "The means of production concerning the variation's theme and its modification in later variations was clearly a model for me." Skoryk's *Variations for Piano* consists of a theme and six variations. The tonal center appears to be D major but is not diatonic. This melody uses alternative modal tones: for example, the lowered third scale degree (F-natural) and the raised fourth scale degree (G-sharp), about which Skoryk says, "This scalar formation is characteristic in Prokofiev's music." A deviation into distant tonalities filled with diatonic references is heard in mm. 5-8 of the theme.

Example 2.21, Myroslav Skoryk, *Piano Variations*, mm. 1-8

The chromatic inflections are clearly associated with Ukrainian melos, where the raised IV scale degree (G-sharp in this instance) is emphasized at the end of each melodic unit in measures 3, 5 and 11 (enharmonically A-flat; see p. 17 no. 3).

Example 2.22, Myroslav Skoryk, *Piano Variations*, mm. 13-20

The prominent reiteration of G-sharp is again heard in the theme's final chord in m. 19. This cadential move to the G-sharp in m. 19 is a result of a three-bar extension originating in the first three measures. Therefore, the phrase structure of the theme can be viewed as 8 + 8 with the extension leading to the G-sharp in mm. 17-19.

Skoryk says, "The first variation, [m. 20] as in classical form, does not travel far from the main theme." Despite its chromaticism, the tonal center remains D while the tempo quickens (*più mosso*) and features syncopation prominently.

Example 2.23, Myroslav Skoryk, *Piano Variations*, Var. 1: mm. 21-24

The second variation (m. 61) continues growing faster with another *più mosso* indication and its tonal center changes to B-flat. Texturally, the variation uses the theme interchangeably between the left and right hands.

Example 2.24, Myroslav Skoryk, *Piano Variations*, Var. 2: mm. 61-68

The third variation (with a mode shift to B-flat minor) introduces a genre element, which is also conventional in classical variation: the construction of march-like rhythms.

Example 2.25, Myroslav Skoryk, *Piano Variations*, Var. 3: mm. 113-124

The fourth variation, a traditionally slow lyric variation, has a firm tonal base in F minor. Skoryk states, "This variation is perhaps the richest in the cycle due to its theme, which is interlaced with inner melodies, sometimes sad in nature along with agogic shifts, chord pulsations and consonant harmonies."

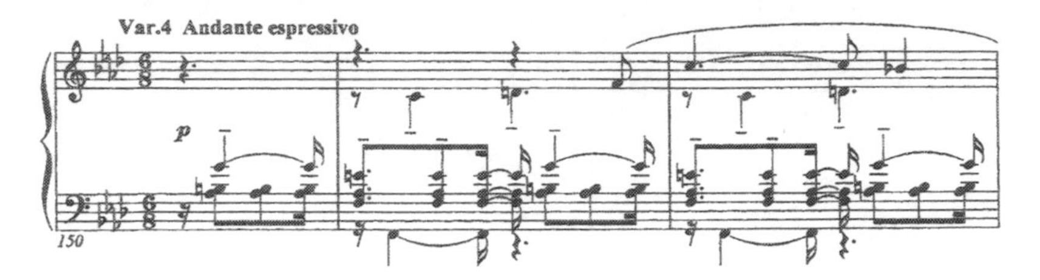

Example 2.26, Myroslav Skoryk, *Piano Variations*, Var. 4: mm. 150-152

In this cycle, Skoryk invests his lyrical character with a certain melancholy, which is typical of Slavic music. Perhaps subconsciously, Skoryk uses the Huculian mode (see p. 18 no. 7), which becomes explicit in the last four measures of this variation. If all notes in mm. 171-172 are written out, this mode is obtained.

Example 2.27, Huculian Mode

Example 2.28, Myroslav Skoryk, *Piano Variations*, Var. 4: mm. 171-172

The first four variations follow a conventional Classical period scheme; but in the fifth variation, Skoryk departs from the traditional plan. "The listener expects the fifth variation to be in a fast tempo with dance-like rhythms and a coda, as is the case in Beethoven's F Major Variations Op. 34." Instead Skoryk constructs the fifth variation differently by composing a funeral march. Accordingly, the key signature is E-flat minor, the lowered second and most obscure key in comparison to the opening main theme in D. Throughout the background of chord sonorities which imitate funeral bells, an expressive theme rises up which gradually accumulates tension and creates sonorous space.

Example 2.29, Myroslav Skoryk, *Piano Variations*, Var. 5: mm. 173-178

The harmonic culmination occurs in mm. 209-211, again building from the combination of three-note chords in E-flat minor and D major; their simultaneous sounds die away on the long fermata (see Example 2.30).

Example 2.30, Myroslav Skoryk, *Piano Variations*, Var. 5: mm. 209-211

The reminiscence of the main theme is heard at the beginning of the sixth variation (in E-flat Minor) continuing on harmonies from variation five combining the E-flat Minor key with the opening D-Major key by way of the reiterated open fifth D-A in both the bass and treble range. This combination of E-flat minor and the pitches D-A throughout mm. 211-222 forms the Huculian mode, now on E-flat.

Example 2.31, Huculian Mode on E-flat (see score Example 2.32 below)

The F-sharp (with bass D-A) in the melody at the end of m. 218 re-establishes the original theme in D while the left hand continues its back and forth striking of the E-flat minor chord and the D-A dyad. Skoryk described the ending as follows: "The first theme is heard as the final sad statement and withers away into space." Similar endings abound in Skoryk's works, specifically his 2nd, 3rd, and 4th Violin Concertos, and *Blues* for piano solo. These endings form a link to his "final recitative solo" previously seen in his *Prelude*.

Example 2.32, Myroslav Skoryk, *Piano Variations*, Var. 6: mm. 212-222

Despite Skoryk's reliance on earlier stylistic models and harmonic vocabulary, his early works show the beginning of many hallmark features evident in his later works. The utilization of jazz rhythms and harmonies, indigenous folk material from Ukraine's Carpathian region and modal material in general provides the genesis for more mature works. The influence of Bartók's music on Skoryk ((0167) in Skoryk's piece "*In the Forest*" from his cycle *In the Carpathians*) would become more pronounced in his 1963 work *Burlesque* of which the so-called "Bartók" trichord (016) plays a significant intervallic and motivic role. The technique of chromatically "filling-in" a larger interval in melodic material and themes (a hallmark of Bartók's music) would gradually take on a more dominant role in Skoryk's thematic material. The "recitative ending" as seen in Skoryk's *Prelude* and *Variations for Piano* would also become a recurring trademark in works to follow. Taken together, the above-mentioned techniques become standard features not only in the solo piano works of Skoryk, but in many of his other works as well.

Works from the 1960s—General Analysis

Blues (1963)

Blues is a short piece representing the time in Skoryk's life when the composer says, "I was interested in the rich expressive possibilities of jazz." In this spirit, Skoryk treats this as a serious piece with the intention of exploiting these expressive elements. Skoryk imitates the freedom and unconstrained trademarks of blues playing, along with suggestions of improvisatory rhythm alternating between the time signatures 6/4 and 4/4 (with a bit of 3/4 introduced as well).

The piece starts in 6/4, about which Skoryk says, "The meter of 6/4 gives me more freedom of pulsation realized in the repetition of dotted rhythmic figures of the accompaniment." Over this accompaniment is stated a whimsical melody at first with little movement but suddenly opening up in m. 6 into a typical jazz solo.

Example 2.33, Myroslav Skoryk, *Blues*, mm. 1-7

Other typical blues features include the walking bass, which supports the extended dotted rhythm of the melody line beginning at m. 18. This leads to the common blues voicing in tenths in the bass (mm. 22-24) followed by the "stride" pattern in tenths in mm. 24-25 (see Example 2.34).

Example 2.34, Myroslav Skoryk, *Blues*, mm. 18-25

The composer's aim is not to imitate any particular blues tune, but to provide a vision of the feeling of the blues, along with exploiting its expressive possibilities. Skoryk states, "My intent is to be successful in providing a picture of the blues not in a folkloric quality but in its general variability." The general structure of the melodic lines shows the character of the composer's style, in particular the connection between major and minor seconds used to fill in chromatic space. This use of chromatic filigree is most notable in mm. 35-37.

Example 2.35, Myroslav Skoryk, *Blues*, mm. 35-37

Harmonically, the minor mode takes precedence in Skoryk's *Blues*; however, Skoryk's ability to mix minor chords with prominent major thirds of the same chord in the arpeggiated melody (or, at m. 30, different qualities of chordal fifths), creates an off-kilter effect as heard in mm. 29-34.

Example 2.36, Myrsolav Skoryk, *Blues*, mm. 29-34

The last bars of *Blues* once again show the recitative-like figure previously discussed regarding the ending of Skoryk's pieces *Prelude*, *Piano Variations*, and the *Violin Concertos 3, 4 and 5*.

Example 2.37, Myroslav Skoryk, *Blues*, mm. 42-44

The dissonant minor second clash (G-sharp/A and D-sharp/E) on the downbeat of m. 42 finally resolves to the A tonality by way of the open fifth A-E in m. 44. Once again this minor second interval and its emphasis at the end of the composition show a hallmark trait of Skoryk.

Within this generally slender, delicate piece, Kyianovska affirms: "*Blues* shows the first attempts in Ukrainian professional music to turn toward jazzy stylistic elements within the limits of modern contemporary music" (Kyianovska p. 41).

Cycle of pieces: *From the Children's Album* (1966)

This small piano cycle for children consists of five pieces:

1. *Prosten'ka melodiia—A Simple Melody*
2. *Narodnyi tanets'—Folk Dance*
3. *Estradna pisnia—Pop Song*
4. *Lirnyk—The Lyre (Hurdy-Gurdy) Player*
5. *Zhartivlyva pisnia—A Humorous Piece*

This cycle has become very popular throughout Ukraine in the pedagogical practice of piano teachers. In these pieces the composer again combines characteristics of folk and jazz music, including the use of modes, which helps invigorate the musical language.

In *A Simple Melody*, the melody stated in the right hand suggests G Mixolydian. However, the opening sonority of C-E-G—coupled with the left-hand pedal point on C—conveys a subtle but unmistakable C Major "priority" colored by inner-voice whole tone successions.

Example 2.38, Myroslav Skoryk, *A Simple Melody*, mm. 1-5

The combination of the right-hand modal and left-hand whole-tone collections produces a polymodal fusion. The ending is uncommon in the sense that it stops in mid-phrase at m. 12 (replicating m. 2) with the notes C, F-Sharp, and A of the diminished chord. This chord recalls the opening statement and its pitch members' function like vii° (F-sharp) to the tonic G (Mixolydian) with the C as tonic pedal point in C Major.

Example 2.39, Myroslav Skoryk, *A Simple Melody*, mm. 11-12

The second piece, *Folk Dance*, as the title indicates, originates in the rhythm of the Carpathian dance. This small rondo form utilizes syncopated melodic rhythms, which imitate characteristic dance motions. The basic tonality is A minor but the melody uses a mode with the raised fourth (D#) and sixth (F#) degrees in m. 1 and 7 (see p. 17 no. 3 and p. 18 no. 4) as well as chordal accompaniment with the lowered sixth degree (F-natural) in mm. 1-3, 6-8 and the lowered second degree B-flat in m. 6. This mode used in the left hand is very similar to the Phrygian mode with its lowered second scale degree (see p. 18 no. 5 and 6).

Example 2.40, Myroslav Skoryk, *Folk Dance*, mm. 1-8

If folk elements prevail in the piece *Folk Dance*, then the following piece *Pop Song* uses typical blues rhythms and Carpathian mode features. The opening sixteen-measure phrase follows the typical 16-bar blues with its I-IV-I V-I harmonic movement. *Pop Song* is also constructed with polyrhythms. The melody (right hand) part is in 3/4 and the left-hand accompaniment, although notated in 3/4, feels like a 6/8 meter. Skoryk reflected on this by saying, "The left hand is designed to sound and feel as if in 6/8 without accents, and the right hand melody in 3/4 meter features a strong syncopation. Together, they produce a swaying-rocking feel characteristic of jazz music." Although the melody suggests the tonality of G major, Skoryk uses a mode with an augmented 2nd between scale degrees 1-2 and the raised fourth scale degree (see p. 18 no. 6).

Example 2.41, Myroslav Skoryk, *Pop Song*, mm. 1-6

The middle section (with the 4/4 meter change setting up the bass line) beginning at m. 17 is more open to jazz qualities in that the left hand imitates a walking bass line. The right hand in m. 17 uses the lowered seventh Mixolydian mode on C.

Example 2.42, Myroslav Skoryk, *Pop Song*, mm. 15-24

The recapitulation at m. 25 is supported by the additional melodic material in mm. 27 and 28, which comes from the middle section material beginning in m. 17. The most apparent similarity is the double note (double third) configuration, which gives the recapitulation the previous jazzy, bluesy mood found in the middle section.

Example 2.43, Myroslav Skoryk, *Pop Song*, mm. 25-28

Measures 41-44 show the integration of both the original melody and the double notes of the middle section. This time the interval of a fourth in the right hand, and in parallel motion, is used as a brief coda.

Example 2.44, Myroslav Skoryk, *Pop Song*, mm. 41-44

The fourth piece in this set, *The Lyre* (Hurdy-Gurdy) *Player,* intends, as Skoryk states, "to represent a folk artist who plays the Lyre." This piece strongly evokes the lyre player turning its wheel resulting in the plucking of the lower strings tuned to a fifth and the right hand providing melodic phrases with the performer singing. As Skoryk describes, the performers were "usually older men, singing historical songs of the past, songs of the audacious Cossack crusades, or battles that they won or lost." The raised fourth (A#) and sixth (C#) scale degrees are found throughout the melody (see p. 17 no. 3).

Example 2.45, Myroslav Skoryk, *The Lyre Player*, mm.1-4

Each new statement of the theme introduces some change or variation in the melody and rhythm as well as an increase dynamically from *piano* at m. 1, to *fortissimo* in m. 53. At m. 29 the theme has modulated a fifth higher in both bass and melody and a canon at the octave at the time interval of one measure begins.

Example 2.46, Myroslav Skoryk, *The Lyre Player*, mm. 29-32

The theme reaches its culmination point in m. 53 marked *fortissimo* with parallel fifths, imitation and dissonant chords.

Example 2.47, Myroslav Skoryk, *The Lyre Player*, mm. 52-55

The re-echoing of the theme's return in m. 61 occurs in a still higher register, only now the dynamic level is much softer with imitation between the hands (now at two measures) at m. 61, 63 and m. 65, 67.

Example 2.48, Myroslav Skoryk, *The Lyre Player*, mm. 60-67

Skoryk described the ending (see Ex. 2.49 mm. 71-77) in this way: "The melody drifts away vanishing into the distant horizon, similar to the reminiscence, which gets lost without a trace." An obvious reference can be drawn between Skoryk's *The Lyre Player* and Schubert's "*Der Leiermann*" from his song cycle *Der Winterreise*.

Example 2.49, Myroslav Skoryk, *The Lyre Player*, mm. 71-77

The final piece in this set, *A Humorous Piece*, is constructed with a balance between folk and jazz elements. Here again Skoryk uses the #4, #6 mode. Generally speaking, the outer sections of this ternary piece (mm. 1-16 and mm. 39-51) are dominated by folk elements with the humorous association showing itself in the changing syncopated accentuations in the melody line, implying a vision of a drunkard. *A Humorous Piece* is rather *buffo* in style, with sharp accents imitating drum beats sounding the interval of fourths and fifths, and chords doubling the theme creating a picture of grotesque play.

Example 2.50, Myroslav Skoryk, *A Humorous Piece*, mm. 1-6

The middle section (mm. 17-32) uses typical elements found in jazz, such as dotted and syncopated rhythms and perfect fifths in the accompaniment (see Example 2.51).

Example 2.51, Myroslav Skoryk, *A Humorous Piece*, mm. 17-21

The decorative embellishment of the dissonant acciaccatura (G-sharp/A) in mm. 48-49 and 51 adds to the humorous play.

Example 2.52, Myroslav Skoryk, *A Humorous Piece*, mm. 48-51

As is evident, this volume combines childlike innocence and emotional openness with a modern piano writing style. Skoryk uses decorative dissonance with a variety of syncopated rhythms and freely improvised rhythmic design. Skoryk has said of this cycle, "Its aim is to establish in children a comprehension and feelings of national style according to the constant pulse of art and teach them intonational discoveries of the twentieth century." Undoubtedly, Skoryk was influenced by Bartók's earlier work for children, the six-volume *Mikrokosmos*.

Works from the 1970s—General Analysis

***Partita No. 5* (1975)**

The *Partita No. 5*, Skoryk's longest solo piano work, ranks among the most popular and frequently played piano works by this composer. Skoryk uses this genre title as he explains "I often use this variant [Partita] and attribute it to the Suite which contains program names such as *Prelude*, *Toccata*, *Aria*, *Waltz*, *Dance*, and *Passacaglia* among others." Skoryk's *Partitas* are written for a combination of instruments and performers as well as for instrumental solo. A list of partitas by Skoryk includes:

Partita No. 1; for String Orchestra
Partita No. 2; for Strings, Woodwinds and Percussion
Partita No. 3; for String Quartet (with a version for String Orchestra)
Partita No. 4; for Symphony Orchestra
Partita No. 5; for Piano Solo
Partita No. 6; for String Quartet (with a version for String Orchestra)
Partita No. 7; for Wind Quintet (with a version for String Orchestra)

Partita No. 5 for piano solo is subtitled "In Modo Retro"—"In Old Style." It consists of five movements titled *Prelude*, *Waltz*, *Chorus*, *Aria* and *Finale*. It is important to note that this partita has a different character in comparison to other works of the composer. It was written in 1975 and seems to follow one of the prominent paths in which music was developing towards the end of the twentieth century. It deals with what Skoryk labels "stylish games [polystylism] and post-modernism, very fashionable at this time." Skoryk goes on to say "Post-

Modernism declares the possibilities of unification of the un-unified, a paradoxical cohabitation of musical styles contained in a work covering diverse extremes of musical material borrowed from different centuries and styles." A detailed analysis of the *Partita No. 5* remains beyond the scope of this overview section. Therefore, I will focus on three prominent and recurring features: first, the deliberate reference to past styles; second, quotation and cross-reference within each movement; and third, the strategic employment of virtuosity.

Skoryk's reference to previous styles within each movement of the *Partita No. 5* is in itself a form of quotation. The *Prelude* combines Baroque and twentieth-century techniques and begins with a stereotypical arpeggiated pattern in C major with a characteristic Baroque descending line in the left hand, which begins on the note B3 and comes to rest on G3 in m. 6. This descending line motive is used in the left-hand material of each movement, suggesting its Baroque association. Regarding this opening, Skoryk notes: "This figuration is intentionally reminiscent of some preludes of Bach." At the same time, the general character of this opening is neo-romantic in its expression (see Example 2.53).

Example 2.53, Myroslav Skoryk, *Partita No. 5*—Prelude, mm. 1-6

An immediate answer occurs in Bach-style organ sounds on a pedal point C beginning in m. 7.

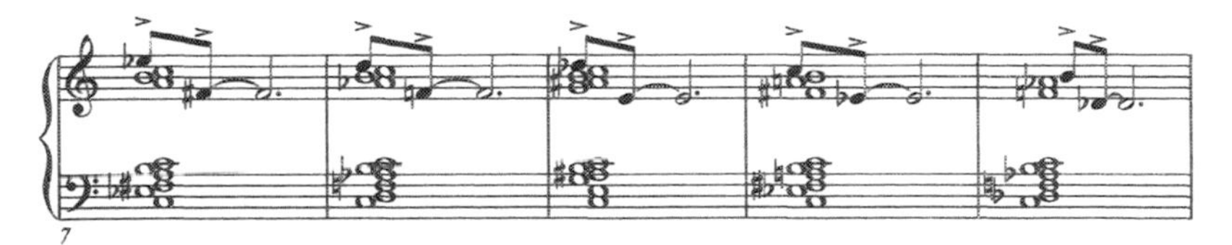

Example 2.54, Myroslav Skoryk, *Partita No. 5*—Prelude, mm. 7-11

A switch from Baroque to twentieth-century style occurs with the succession of dissonant arpeggios encompassing the entire range of the keyboard in mm. 21-22 (the last arpeggio in m. 22 contains all twelve pitch classes in a single sweep) in what Skoryk refers to as "an unexpected dodecaphonic passage."

Example 2.55, Myroslav Skoryk, *Partita No. 5*—Prelude, mm. 21-22

In this opening movement Skoryk fuses Baroque and twentieth-century attributes such as the descending bass line, organ pedal points, and consistent sequential figuration. These materials are presented in an eclectic fusion of neo-baroque and neo-romantic manners.

Like the *Prelude*, the *Waltz* is clearly a mixture of different styles. When writing this movement, Skoryk had in mind waltzes by Ravel, Tchaikovsky, and Strauss. The opening eight-measure phrase utilizes the light syncopation of a *Ländler* [waltz] with its short-long rhythmic accentuation along with hemiola. An unexpected meter change to 4/4 in m. 7 gives the feeling of what Skoryk calls "a rhythmic swell" switching back to 3/4 in m. 8, thus completing the phrase and leading to a restatement in m. 9.

Example 2.56, Myroslav Skoryk, *Partita No. 5*—Waltz, mm. 1-10

The new theme beginning in m. 17 contains a more typical waltz melody in the style of what Skoryk calls "the *Vienna Waltzes* by Johann Strauss." The *Ländler* waltz short-long accentuation now disappears with the customary strong downbeat of the waltz rhythm taking control.

Example 2.57, Myroslav Skoryk, *Partita No. 5*—Waltz, mm. 16-25

Virtuosic writing is first heard in the brilliant octave passages (in quasi Lisztian style) in two waves between mm. 61-72, followed by a stylistic switch to jazz harmonies which accompany melodic arpeggios in mm. 73-78 (see Example 2.58).

Example 2.58, Myroslav Skoryk, *Partita No. 5*—Waltz, mm. 61-78

Another example of virtuosity occurs in m. 94 where a frenzied, boisterous waltz theme reminiscent of Ravel's *La Valse* erupts as Skoryk explains: "This passage evokes a kind of applied music for band orchestra with the dynamic marked *fortissimo*." The technical difficulty here lies in the spacious and rapid octave left-hand jumps on the downbeat of each bar with beats two and three containing four and five-note octave chords.

Example 2.59, Myroslav Skoryk, *Partita No. 5*—Waltz, mm. 95-104

The third movement, *Chorus*, is constructed from two contrasting elements: the basic texture of the chorale (mm. 1-3); and the following arpeggiation in m. 4, borrowed from the opening arpeggios of the *Prelude* movement. Kyianovska describes this dual as follows: "The rigidity of the dissonant chord statements is contrasted with fluttering improvisational virtuosic arpeggios first occurring in the *Prelude* . . . intervallic discord as well as chord dissonances transfer stylistic sources into a modern platform" (Kyianovska p. 119). Measures 1-5 show the juxtaposition between these two contrasting elements (see Example 2.60).

Example 2.60, Myroslav Skoryk, *Partita No. 5*—Chorus, mm. 1-5

The fourth movement, *Aria*, is more consistent in its style. However, this *Aria* contains what Skoryk calls "more sentimental and banal idioms" which instantly communicate the effect of the composer's mockery of this style. The general style of melody and accompaniment (with its descending bass line) conjures up a spirit similar to that of Chopin's pianistic style.

Example 2.61, Myroslav Skoryk, *Partita No. 5*—Aria, mm. 1-12

The cross-reference to the *Prelude* and the *Chorale* motive is achieved by the accented and reiterated octave and octave/minor 2nd dissonance in mm. 38ff (see also Example 2.53 and 2.60). Virtuosity in fluency of double-note technique and, in particular, legato triadic figuration in the left hand takes precedence between mm. 46-49 (see Example 2.62).

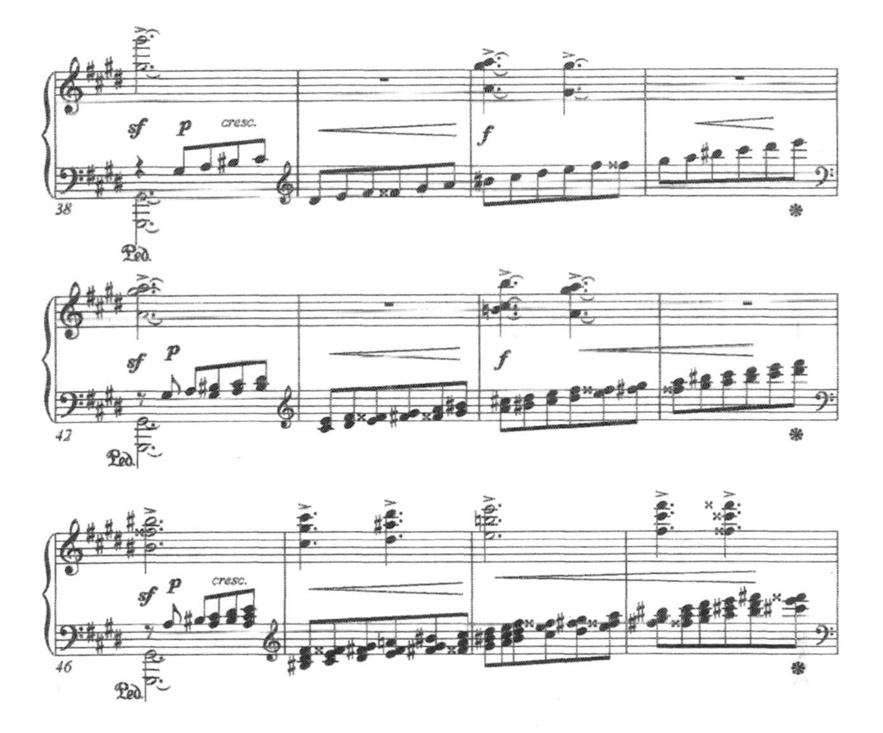

Example 2.62, Myroslav Skoryk, *Partita No. 5*—Aria, mm. 38-49

The lengthy *Finale* is constructed on what Kyianovska calls "the juxtaposition of two contrasting episodes which alternate in kaleidoscopic speed and brevity" (Kyianovska p. 120). The most interesting feature of this *Finale* is how the composer uses thematic material from previous movements and incorporates it into the movement. In her article, Marta Vovk says, "The *Finale* contains a mixture of different micro-episodes such as a march, jazz, and features of different stylistic periods in addition to thematic elements from previous movements" (Yakubiak p. 73). This borrowing of material from previous movements helps to unite the *Finale*.

The inherent whimsicality of the thematic material in this movement combines with the composer's use of quotation—from himself and other composers—as a fitting form of parody. The type of quotation technique used by Skoryk is accurately described by Elliott Schwartz as follows: "Quotations from other music may be brief and fleeting, drawn from relatively obscure works, or so carefully disguised that immediate recognition is unlikely. In any event, the quotations are not necessarily central to the primary argument of the work" (Schwartz p. 251).

When using quotations in his music, Skoryk consistently incorporates them into the style of the composition at hand. In this way, Skoryk's ability to fuse different styles coincides with Schwartz' idea: "The borrowed material has been "translated" into the language of the composer and treated in a manner consistent with that language, thus maintaining a sense of stylistic uniformity" (Schwartz p. 243). In this way, Skoryk differs from a composer like Alfred Schnittke who often uses quotations in sharp stylistic contrast within his works. Schwartz sums up this phenomenon: "Recent decades have seen a proliferation of works in which borrowed materials are deliberately treated as isolated fragments from the 'outside world' that clash with the prevailing style rather than conform to it" (Schwartz p. 243).

The *Finale's* formal layout consists of a hybrid rondo design shown below in Figure 2.1. Within this movement, Skoryk's primary focus is on virtuosic piano technique and the quotation of both borrowed material (in the first part of the movement, mm. 1-88) followed by self-quotation (cross-reference to previous movements) in the second half (mm. 89-155).

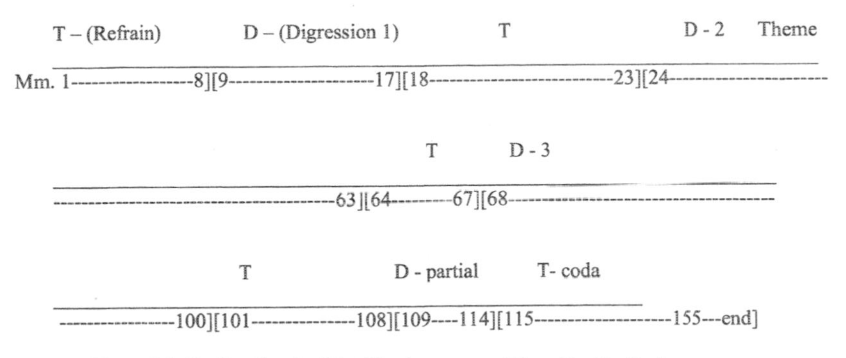

Figure 2.1, Outline Graph of the *Finale* movement from *Partita No.5*

The opening refrain material in mm. 1-8 contains rapid scale runs followed by accented chords, which feature the piano technique of contraction versus expansion.

Example 2.63, Myroslav Skoryk, *Partita No. 5*—Finale, mm. 1-8

Beginning in m. 9, the first episode continues with rapid scale passages that pass through a technically demanding repeated-note passage in m. 12 and lead to the brief quotation of *Santa Claus is Coming to Town* (Skoryk describes this passage (mm. 14-15) as a "banal jazz theme"). This is followed in m. 16 by a quote of the opening to Chopin's *Etude* in F Major Op. 10 No. 8.

Example 2.64, Myroslav Skoryk, *Partita No. 5*—Finale, mm. 9-16

The refrain theme returns in m. 19 and in parody Skoryk uses a fragment of the former USSR anthem transformed into a rapid march-like contortion in mm. 23-24. This leads to the second episode in m. 25, which begins, with so-called symphonic unisons—a reference to the opening of Beethoven's *Coriolan* *Overture*.

Example 2.65, Myroslav Skoryk, *Partita No. 5*—Finale, mm. 19-30

The symphonic unisons give way to a dance introduction about which Skoryk says, "A real Gypsy dance begins, and, as is customary, gallops to its furious accelerando." The example below shows how the rhythm intensifies, as Skoryk changes the bass note durations from half notes (mm. 41-47) to eighth note/dotted quarter syncopation at mm. 49-52 and finally virtuosic octave repetitions at mm. 57-63.

Example 2.66, Myroslav Skoryk, *Partita No. 5*—Finale, mm. 41-47

Example 2.67, Myroslav Skoryk, *Partita No. 5*—Finale, mm. 49-52

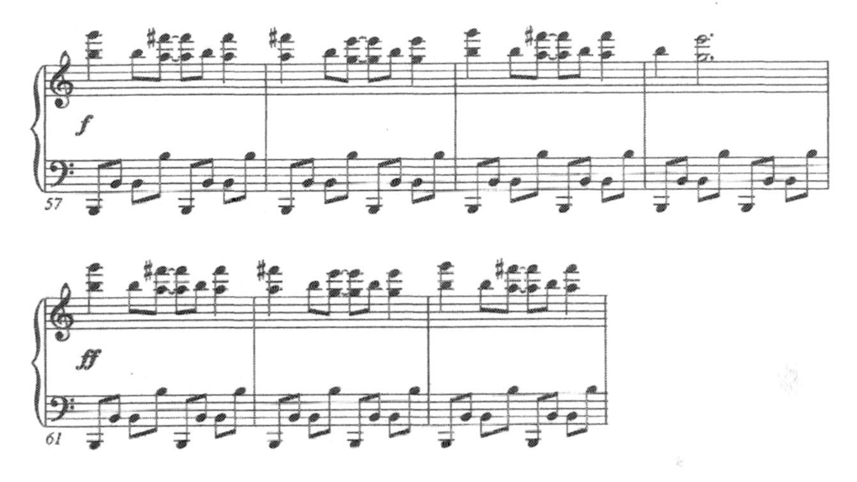

Example 2.68, Myroslav Skoryk, *Partita No. 5*—Finale, mm. 57-63

In the last half of the *Finale*, the cross reference of previous movement material dominates as Skoryk says, "The *Chorale* motive is used in the section between mm. 89 and 108 with a direct quote in mm. 96, 99, 102-103 and 107-109." A short two-measure reference to the refrain theme is embedded in this section between mm. 102-103 and 107-108, thereby juxtaposing the themes from the two respective movements (see Example 2.69).

Example 2.69, Myroslav Skoryk, *Partita No. 5*—Finale, mm. 89-108

Skoryk goes on to say, "The *Aria's* theme is used in mm. 109-110 and a fragment from the *Prelude* in mm. 111-114 ending on the dominant of C, which leads to the refrain coda."

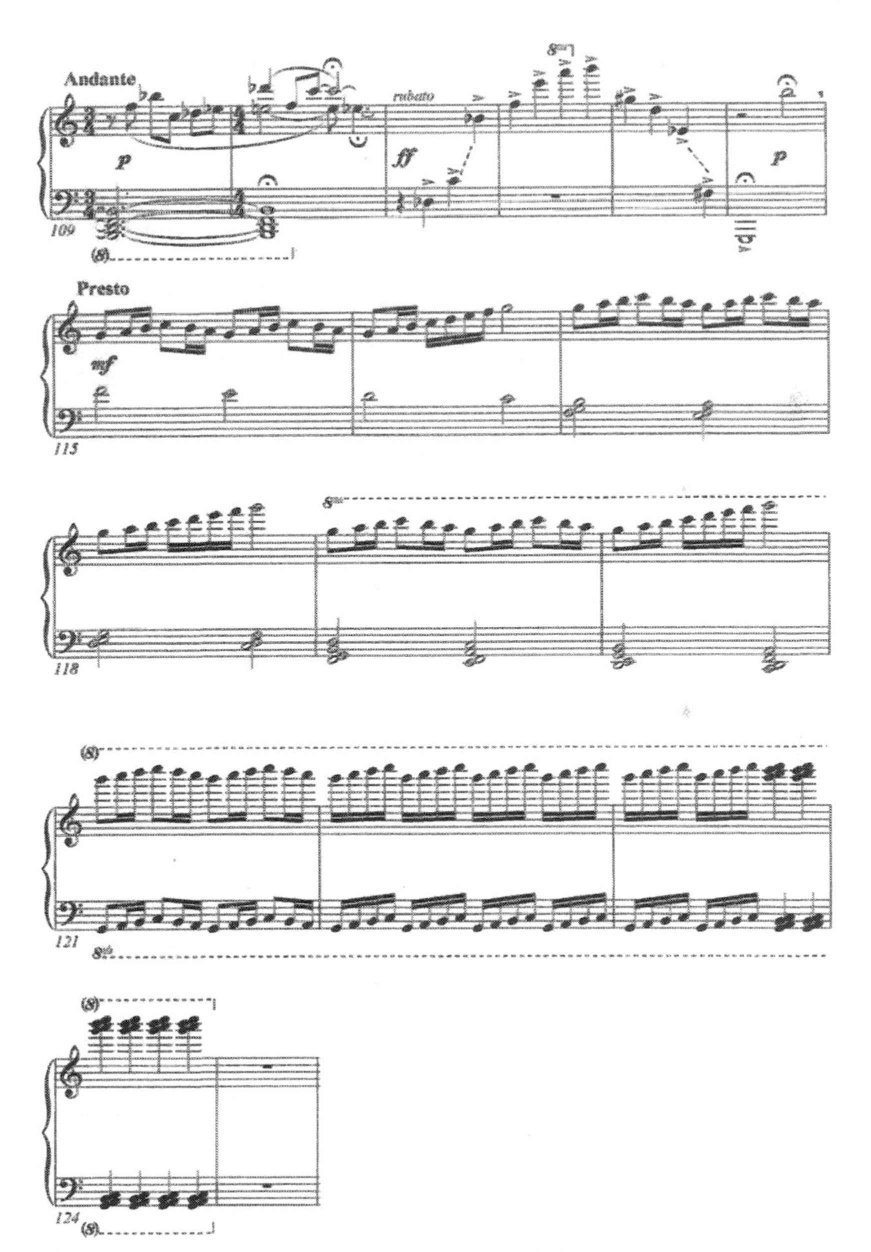

Example 2.70, Myroslav Skoryk, *Partita No. 5*—Finale, mm. 109-125

A brief restatement of the Beethovenian "symphonic unisons" occurs between mm. 126-129, leading to an extended repetition of a C diatonic chord cluster with tied notes held over and alternating between D-minor and E-minor triads. Skoryk notes: "The effect of the coda is to imitate the sound of the harmonica—an unexpected effect."

In summing up this movement, Skoryk utilizes self-quotation by means of cross-reference to previous movements. To carry the idea of quotation a step farther, Skoryk employs the quotation of borrowed material while consistently incorporating it within his harmonic language. This virtuosic piece has taken second place to the *Burlesque* in popularity of Skoryk's solo piano works.

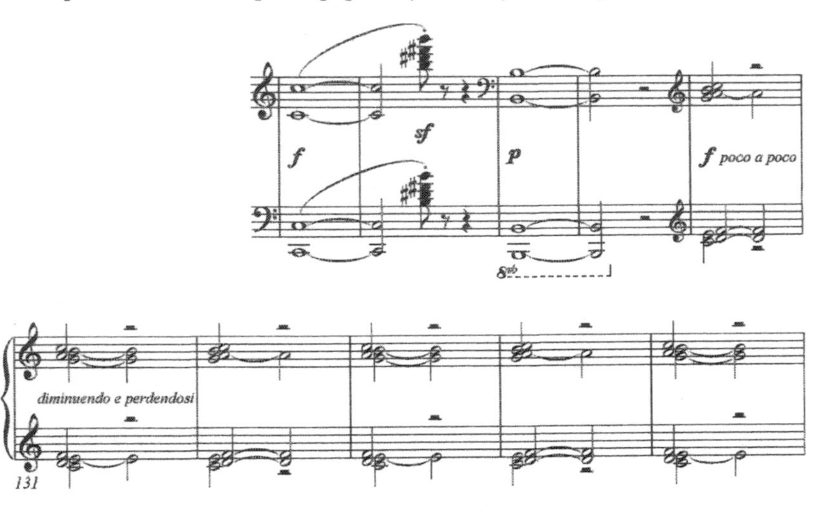

Example 2.71, Myroslav Skoryk, *Partita No. 5*—Finale, mm. 126-135

Toccata (1978)

In describing this work Skoryk says "The *Toccata's* stylistic elements point towards a continuation of my *Burlesque* for piano as well as the finale of the *1st Violin Sonata* and *1st Concerto for Violin*." This work contains some trade-mark features of the composer such as the opening theme's chromatic fill-in of its boundary interval (D-G). Skoryk also composed this work with a focus on virtuosity and play of canonic and mirror imitation. An unexpected feature is the opening theme's alteration of eighth notes by way of metric changes resulting in the following pattern: m. 1—seven eighth notes; m. 2—five; m. 3—six; m. 4—three; m. 5—eight; m. 6—three and so on. This creates an effect of what Skoryk terms "a disintegration of rhythmic pattern." In contrast to a typical rhythmically organized opening episode, this introduction presents an unevenness of accents resulting in a broken texture (see Example 2.72). Regardless of the complex chromaticism and chordal dissonance, the *Toccata* is strongly based in the key of D major, a result of the theme's constant emphasis on the pitch D.

Example 2.72, Myroslav Skoryk, *Toccata*, mm. 1-11

Three main ideas permeate this piece, the first being the opening motive's influence on the structure of the work. The toccata divides into a three-part form as outlined in Figure 2.2.

A A B A

Mm. 1------49—50-----96—97-----165—166-----203

Figure 2.2, Outline form chart of *Toccata*

The opening three notes D, E, and G, ascend to form a similar melodic motive that is used to begin each section of the *Toccata* (see Example 2.73).

Example 2.73, Myroslav Skoryk, *Toccata*, mm. 1, 99, and 166

The second and third ideas feature repeated toccata-like notes throughout this work along with the influence of canonic writing. Measures 34-40 contain repeated F-sharps and mirror chromatic figuration leading to a mirror canon in m. 40 (see Example 2.74).

Example 2.74, Myroslav Skoryk, *Toccata*, mm. 34-40

The repeated F-sharps first heard in m. 34 play a significant role in the contrasting B section material (marked *Meno mosso)* beginning in m. 97. Here, the composer changes to "repetition status" with repeated notes on F-sharp accompanying sporadic triplet figures based on the opening melodic motive (see Example 2.75).

Example 2.75, Myroslav Skoryk, *Toccata*, mm. 97-104

Skoryk's playful games are further summed up by his explanation: "My intention is for this passage [section] to mimic and remind one of the Morse Code Alphabet. . . . Another plaster of recitative order, almost speech like, first restrained, then growing more agitated to a nervous convulsion." This paroxysm is successfully achieved by the registral and dynamic ascent of the "Morse Code" figure beginning in m. 129 on G (marked *Forte sempre*) and climbing chromatically to A-flat in m. 133.

Example 2.76, Myroslav Skoryk, *Toccata*, mm. 127-133

Measure 149 contains the "repetition status" now with F-sharp in the bass and C-sharp in the right hand marked *pianissimo*. Here, C# functions as 5/F# and 7/D.

Example 2.77, Myroslav Skoryk, *Toccata*, mm. 149-152

After a pause at m. 165 the last section (recap) returns to the toccata motion in eighth notes. This section begins with the exact three-note melodic motive, which initiated the B section in m. 99 (and recalls the first three notes of the piece as discussed above). The right hand is in mirror figuration with the left hand as the dynamic level increases (see Example 2.78). The G6 and F6 in mm. 175-176 circle around the axis of F-sharp (3/D) whose *forte* arrival occurs at m. 177. Skoryk confirms, "The F-sharp pitch in this recapitulation section constitutes the third scale degree of the main tonality in D." The fourth beat of mm. 178 and 179 contain the exact opening motive: the pitches, D-E-G (see Examples 2.78 and 2.79).

Example 2.78, Myroslav Skoryk, *Toccata*, mm. 165-176

Example 2.79, Myroslav Skoryk, *Toccata*, mm. 177-179

The ending is almost mirror-like in the sense that Skoryk ends the *Toccata* with a return of the main theme from the opening measures (see Example 2.80).

Example 2.80, Myroslav Skoryk, *Toccata*, mm. 194-203

The *Toccata* is a compact work; its main sectional divisions unified through the use of recurring motives, repeated notes, and canonic writing. The general virtuosity and rhythmic drive have attracted several pianists to add it to their repertoire.

Works from the 1980s—General Analysis

***Six Preludes and Fugues for Piano* (1988)**

This cycle is clearly based on J.S. Bach's "Well Tempered Clavier" and continues the tradition of preludes and fugues by twentieth-century masters Paul Hindemith (*Ludus Tonalis*) and Dmitri Shostakovich (24 Preludes and Fugues). Notwithstanding their differences in tonal language, Skoryk's work follows that of his twentieth-century predecessors in its reliance on traditional contrapuntal techniques. Skoryk notes:

> A rational compactness and constructive linear writing is congenial with neoclassical tendencies in a modern perception of people very distant by their origin. Some analogies present themselves in the usage of a universal counterpoint method, opulence of polyphonic technique and the creation of a certain "polyphonic encyclopedia."

Skoryk projected his cycle to contain a dozen preludes and fugues moving chromatically through the major keys (which Skoryk referred to as a "micro-cycle"); but until now only six have been completed. Thus the key scheme follows the pattern C Major, D-Flat Major, D Major, E-Flat Major, E Major and F Major. Skoryk's use of major and minor modality in the majority of his preludes and fugues is ambiguous. In his polyphonic writing the dissonant nature of his contrapuntal combination of melodies, as well as his limited use of 12-tone themes, take the place of clearly articulated keys and modes.

The obligatory tonal center is established at the beginning of each movement, generally through a strong statement of tonic in the bass. However, this tonal center becomes more ambiguous as the composer treats the material more liberally. Often the orientation of the basic tonality is clearly audible, especially in the form's critical moments. Dissonant harmonies sound as a consequence of purely linear movement in the surrounding voices, which tend to overshadow the tonal center. Consequently, a key signature is omitted for each movement, although Skoryk indicates the key in the title of each prelude and fugue.

Stylistically, the cycle recalls the "stylistic games" previously discussed in relation to post-modernism. In his use of polystylism, there is a clear analogy to his earlier *Partita No. 5* for piano. Both works feature analogies to different stylistic sources not compatible with Baroque polyphony. Often the expected methods of contrapuntal development are breached by melodic structures hinting at styles as diverse as dodecaphony and jazz. Nevertheless, Skoryk's *Preludes and Fugues* show an overall wholeness and stylistic, harmonic, and modal unity.

This integrity resides in the highly varied development of one main thematic idea in each prelude and fugue.

Skoryk's *Preludes and Fugues* utilize all the trademarks of Baroque polyphonic technique. The preludes typically utilize a rhythmic and/or melodic motive, which is developed throughout the piece. An interesting example is the *Prelude No. 2* in D-flat, which is based almost entirely on the imitation of bells. The prelude starts with a one-measure ostinato figure reminding us of the popular Ukrainian song "Shchedryk" composed in 1916 by the Ukrainian composer Mykola Leontovych (later adapted and used in the famous song "Carol of the Bells") except that Skoryk uses this theme in the major mode (with rhythmic alteration). This motive is repeated in the first twelve measures and is harmonized with chords built on all twelve pitch classes.

Example 2.81, Myroslav Skoryk, *Prelude No. 2 in D Flat*, mm. 1-12

Example 2.82, "Shchedryk"; original version as written by Mykola Leontovych

Another interesting example is the opening to the fifth *Prelude in E Major*. Here Skoryk begins the piece with a scalar passage repeated in many octaves. This basic theme is then interrupted with a cadential move in mm. 4-6 utilizing the intervallic inversion of the first five notes. These pitches in the right hand Db-Eb-E-F#-G#, spell the relative (enharmonic) minor of the E major opening (see Example 2.83).

Example 2.83, Myroslav Skoryk, *Prelude No. 5 in E Major*, mm. 1-7

Skoryk's fugues utilize the polyphonic techniques of inversion, stretto, rhythmic augmentation and diminution, crab, inverted crab, retrograde, and canon. For example, the subject from *Fugue No. 3* (mm. 1-4) is imitated in inversion around the axis of F sharp (mm. 5-8):

Example 2.84, Myroslav Skoryk, *Fugue No. 3*, mm. 1-8

A retrograde occurs in the top voice beginning in m. 9, followed by its inversion in m. 13.

Example 2.85, Myroslav Skoryk, *Fugue No. 3*, m. 9-14; Crab move

The fugue subject from Skoryk's fourth fugue is used later in *stretto*.

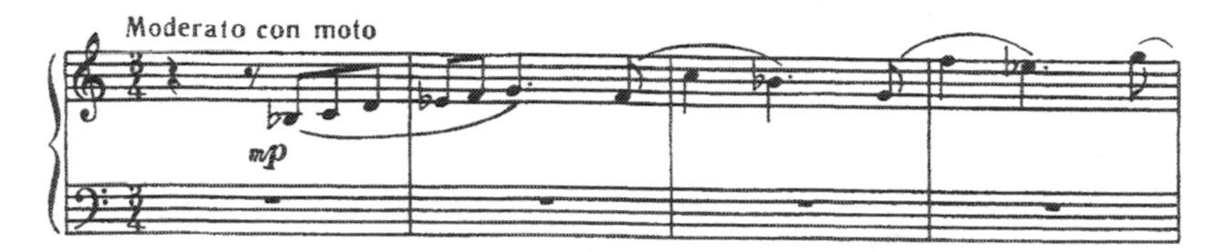

Example 2.86, Myroslav Skoryk, *Fugue No. 4*, mm. 1-4

Example 2.87, Myroslav Skoryk, *stretto* passage from *Fugue No. 4*, mm. 55-60

The passage below from the same fugue is an example of the subject in rhythmic diminution occurring in the bass voice beginning at m. 30.

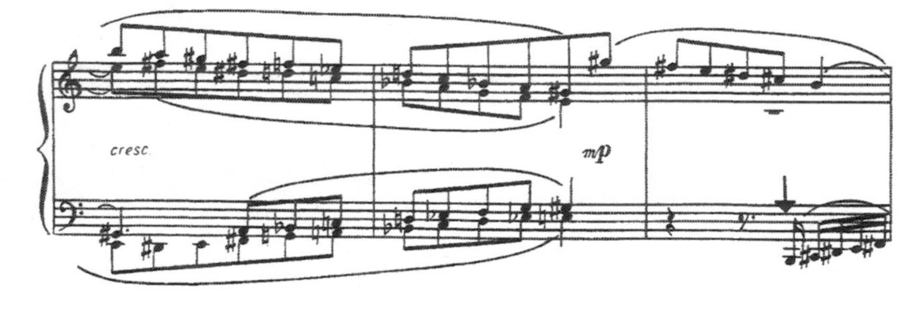

Example 2.88, Myroslav Skoryk, *Fugue No. 4*, mm. 28-33

The subject from the fifth fugue later occurs in the soprano voice in m. 27 with canonic imitation in the middle voice one bar later. This occurs simultaneously with inverted rhythmic augmentation in the bass voice beginning in m. 27.

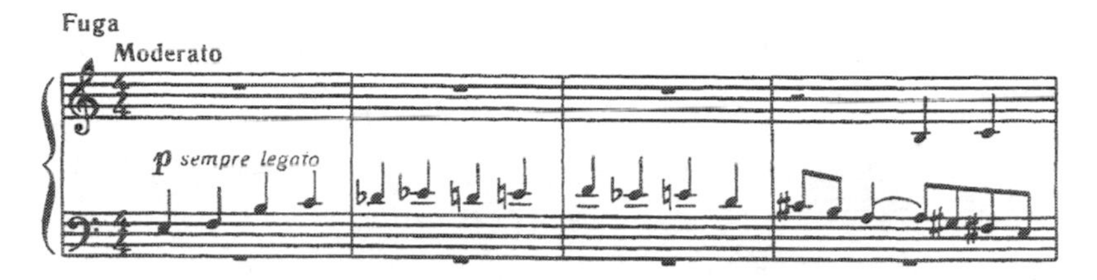

Example 2.89, Myroslav Skoryk, *Fugue No. 5*, mm.1-4; Fugue Subject

Example 2.90, Myroslav Skoryk, *Fugue No. 5*, mm. 26-30

Finally, the subject from the sixth fugue in F major is reminiscent of what Skoryk calls “a playful children’s song” evoking a jazz feeling.

Example 2.91, Myroslav Skoryk, *Fugue No. 6*, mm. 1-8

Later, Skoryk utilizes the technique of an extended pedal point passage constructed with the subject's fifth interval in order to re-establish the F-major tonality.

Example 2.92, Myroslav Skoryk, *Fugue No. 6*, mm. 58-63

This last statement of the subject beginning at m. 80 is disguised with jazz harmonies and sounded twice in fortissimo gradually diminishing in dynamics.

Example 2.93, Myroslav Skoryk, *Fugue No. 6*, mm. 75-89

The last three measures are a coda-like statement marked *rubato*, leading chromatically to an unexpected F-sharp minor chord over the bass F-natural. Evidently, this chord is what Skoryk summarizes as "a harmony that represents a link to the next prelude and fugue in this cycle, which regretfully, I have not yet written" (see Example 2.93, mm. 87-89).

In general, this cycle of preludes and fugues by Myroslav Skoryk is marked with liveliness, catchy themes, and unforeseen contrasts in quite normative forms. Skoryk says regarding this cycle, "The pianistic writing has given way to its popularity among concert pianists as well as teachers [who use the preludes and fugues] as pedagogical material."

Works from the 1990s–General Analysis

***Six Jazz pieces for Piano* (1993)**

The six pieces in the cycle are titled as follows:

1. *In Ukrainian Folk Style*
2. *Reiterating Tune*
3. *Pleasant Stroll*
4. *Caprice*
5. *In an Old Jazz Style*
6. *Arabesque*

Here the composer's intent is to combine jazz style, Ukrainian folk material and his own melodic and harmonic peculiarities. Skoryk achieves his goal by combining several different elements including Ukrainian Carpathian melodies, walking bass, stride, syncopation, suggestions of "trading licks" between ensemble and soloist, the typical jazz voicing of octave with fifth, and harmonic/melodic exchange by way of register shifts. Each piece is constructed in what Skoryk describes as "a traditional jazz piece: theme, with its several variations."

Skoryk's six jazz pieces begin with the typical thirty-two bar song form, or a shortening of this form in *Reiterating Tune* and *Pleasant Stroll*. In addition, the end of each piece states the theme or some variation thereof with the exception of *In an Old Jazz Style*. The first piece, *In Ukrainian Folk Style*, uses a theme which originates from Ukrainian Carpathian violin melodies and dances with modal characteristics: the raised fourth and sixth scale degrees in A minor as well as the use of the lowered seventh scale degree in major (see p. 17 no. 2 and no. 3). Figure 2.3 shows the outline of this song form.

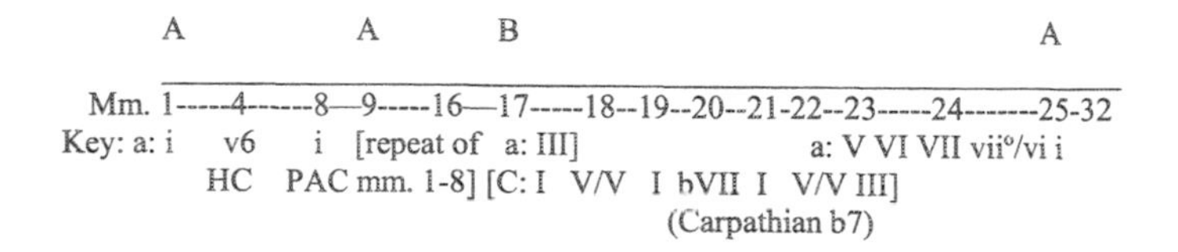

Figure 2.3, *In Ukrainian Folk Style*, outline of theme

The theme or head consists of an eight-measure phrase, 4+4 in A minor. The antecedent phrase leads to a half cadence at m. 4 followed by a perfect authentic cadence ending the consequent phrase in m. 8. Measures 9-16 are an exact repeat of the first phrase. Measures 17-24, in C major, constitute the bridge section. The return to A minor in m. 25 is a restatement of the head (A) theme (mm. 25-32). Mark Gridley summarizes the thirty-two bar song form as follows: "The thirty-two bar tune is made up of four eight-measure sections. The opening eight measures, called the A section, is repeated in the second section. The third part is the B section, sometimes referred to as the bridge, release, inside, or channel. The last eight measures (mm. 25-32) are a repeat of the opening eight measures. The tune falls into what is called AABA form" (Gridley p. 378). When describing the bridge, Gridley writes "The B section of an AABA tune . . . bridges the gap between repetition of A sections, and it usually provides a contrast to the material in the A sections. The bridge can break up or lift the mood established by repeated A sections. Many bridges are placed a few keys higher than the A section. A key change can be a boost in any situation, but especially effective after the repeated A sections" (Gridley p. 386). In this way, Skoryk modulates to C major in m. 17; however, the music avoids going to the dominant of C, instead moving through major triads in (mostly) whole steps until the return of V/A minor in m. 23 preceding the reprise. Example 2.94 shows the opening twenty-five measures (AAB) of *In Ukrainian Folk Style*.

Example 2.94, Myroslav Skoryk, *In Ukrainian Folk Style*, mm. 1-25

In Ukrainian Style contains one lengthy variation (mm. 33-110), which is divided into four sections, each of which is based on the employment of various textural/figurative techniques (see Figure 2.4).

<u>Jazz piece #1, *In Ukrainian Folk Style*</u>

Var. I: Mm. 33-110

Section 1 Mm. 33-72	Section 2 Mm. 73-80
Section 3 Mm. 81-96	Section 4 Mm. 97-110

Figure 2.4, Variation outline for *In Ukrainian Folk Style*

The first section (mm. 33-72) contains five symmetrical eight-measure phrases alternating between A minor and C major and features a steady "on the beat" triadic accompaniment (L.H.) to the syncopated melodic line in the right hand (see Example 2.95).

Example 2.95, Myroslav Skoryk, *In Ukrainian Folk Style*, mm. 33-40

The second section, (mm. 73-80) switches over to a typical jazz octave with fifth chord texture (and tremolo figuration) in the right hand over a seventh chord accompaniment in the left (see Example 2.96).

Example 2.96, Myroslav Skoryk, *In Ukrainian Folk Style*, mm. 73-79

Section three, mm. 81-96, utilizes alternating broken octaves, which lead to the fourth and final section between mm. 97-110. This last section features full octave four-note chords in the right hand over left-hand octaves in polyrhythms (see Examples 2.97 and 2.98).

Example 2.97, Myroslav Skoryk, *In Ukrainian Folk Style*, mm. 81-89

Example 2.98, Myroslav Skoryk, *In Ukrainian Folk Style*, mm. 97-104

The theme of the second piece, *Reiterating Tune* (in F-minor) differs from the first piece in that its head (mm. 1-8) is stated in repeated two-measure groups, 2+2+2+2 (hence the piece's title) immediately going into the bridge passage (mm. 9-16), a result of the theme's constant reiteration in mm. 1-8. The left hand of the opening eight-measure phrase recalls the jazz technique of "comping" and what Gridley describes as "accompanying or complementing" the right hand melodic/ thematic material (Gridley p. 18). The opening texture is intended to evoke a typical jazz ensemble with horn section. Measures 17-24 repeat the opening eight measures leading to the first variation in m. 25. Consequently the form of the theme abbreviates the thirty-two bar song form, yielding the 8 x 3 bar ABA form shown below in Figure 2.5. Example 2.99 shows the first sixteen measures.

A B A

Mm. 1-----------------8—9-----------------16—17----------24

exact repeat
of mm. 1-8

Figure 2.5, *Reiterating Tune*, outline of theme

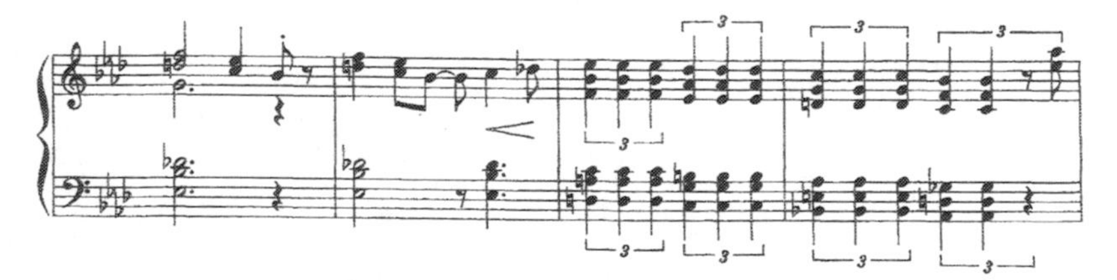

Example 2.99, Myroslav Skoryk, *Reiterating Tune*, mm. 1-16

The full texture of the opening contrasts with the first two variations employing what Skoryk says "a characteristic walking bass." Figure 2.6 shows the measure numbers of each variation as contained in the score.

<u>Jazz piece #2, *Reiterating Tune*</u>

Var. I: Mm. 25-48
Var. II: Mm. 57-78

Figure 2.6, Variation outline for *Reiterating Tune*

Variation I begins with the anacrusis to m. 25 and features a syncopated right-hand melodic line in counterpoint with the left-hand walking bass line. The right hand occasionally utilizes the triplet figuration, which first occurred in the B section (mm. 15-16) of the opening theme (see Example 2.100).

Example 2.100, Myroslav Skoryk, *Reiterating Tune*, Var. I, mm. 24-32

Variation II, beginning in m. 57, continues with the same syncopated melodic line and walking bass figuration as Variation I, but changes over to a typical jazz voicing octave with fifth in the right hand and seventh chords in the left hand in m. 73 (see Examples 2.101 and 2.102).

Example 2.101, Myroslav Skoryk, *In Ukrainian Folk Style*, Var. II, mm. 57-61

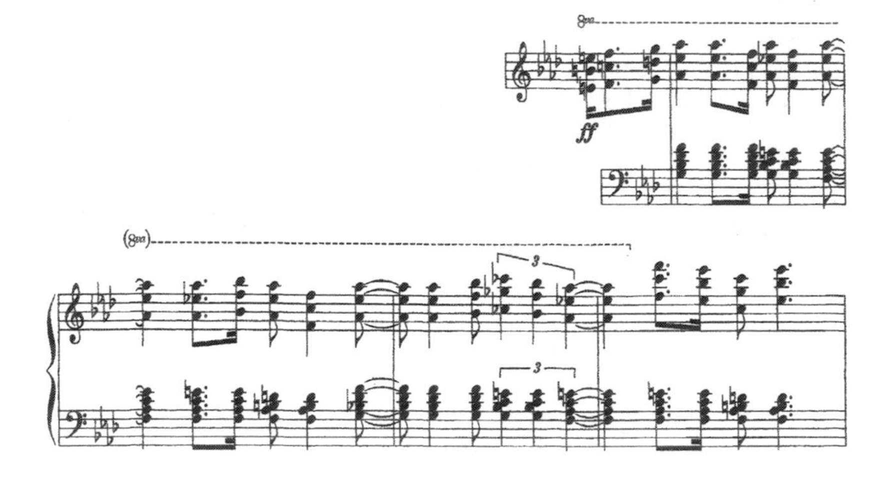

Example 2.102, Myroslav Skoryk, *In Ukrainian Folk Style*, Var. II, mm. 72-76

Pleasant Stroll, in F major, the third piece in this set, is based on an abbreviated sixteen-bar song form. Each phrase is four measures long (with a syncopated melodic line over a walking bass) while the bridge (mm. 9-12) remains in F with contrasting melodic material. The last four measures before Variation I (mm. 13-16) are similar to mm. 1-4; however, a harmonically closed V-I occurs at m. 15, which leads to the anacrusis (m. 16) to variation I (m. 17). Figure 2.7 charts the theme of *Pleasant Stroll*, followed by example 2.103, which shows the opening sixteen measures of the score.

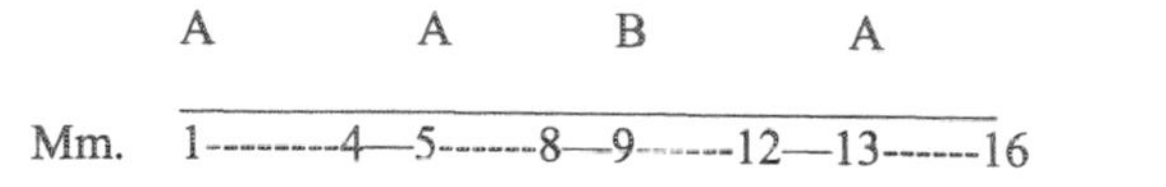

Figure 2.7, *Pleasant Stroll*, outline of theme

Example 2.103, Myroslav Skoryk, *Pleasant Stroll*, mm. 1-16

Figure 2.8 charts each variation.

<u>Jazz piece #3, *Pleasant Stroll*</u>

Var. I: Mm. 17-32
Var. II: Mm. 33-48
Var. III: Mm. 49-64
Var. IV: Mm. 65-79 (Repeat of Var. II)

Figure 2.8, Myroslav Skoryk, *Pleasant Stroll*, mm. 1-16

Variation I, beginning in m. 17, contains double-third figuration in the right hand melodic line over a walking bass comprised of seventh chords. This chord statement replicates the jazz ensemble and the percussion hi-hat. Regarding performance practice beginning m. 17, the pianist should depress the sostenuto pedal on the first and third beats only letting the second and fourth beats remain un-pedaled, thereby bringing to life the intended high-hat percussive effect (see Example 2.104).

Example 2.104, Myroslav Skoryk, *Pleasant Stroll*, mm. 17-20

Measure 33 begins Variation II in responsorial style with the chord tremolo triplet figuration replicating a full jazz horn section (mm. 33-34) followed by the customary solo in mm. 35-36 (see Example 2.105).

Example 2.105, Myroslav Skoryk, *Pleasant Stroll*, mm. 33-36

Beginning in m. 49 (see Example 2.106), the third variation replicates the same texture and figuration of Variation I: a syncopated melodic line over a walking bass. Unusually, Variation IV is an exact repeat of the second variation, but works effectively in leading back to the head theme and giving an overall ternary structure to the piece (see Figure 2.9).

Example 2.106, Myroslav Skoryk, *Pleasant Stroll*, mm. 49-52

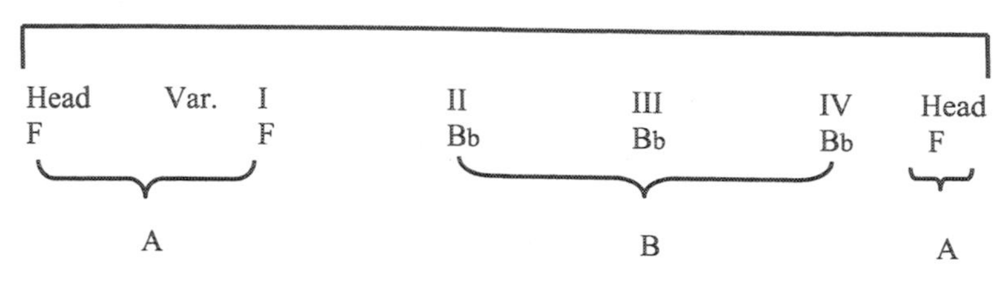

Figure 2.9, Form Outline of *Pleasant Stroll*

The plan in this work seems somewhat redundant in its focus on tonic, dominant and secondary dominant harmonies. However, the composer's creative manipulation of the melodic line lends interest to the piece.

The fourth piece in this cycle, *Caprice*, is constructed as Skoryk states, "on piquant jazz harmonies, saturated with dotted rhythms and syncopations." His piquant harmonies result from the G minor and G Dorian inflection in the melodic line of the head, supported by chord sevenths with added 9ths, 11ths and 13ths, which lead to the dominant D7 and i9 (V-i) chord in mm. 7-8 (see Example 2.107).

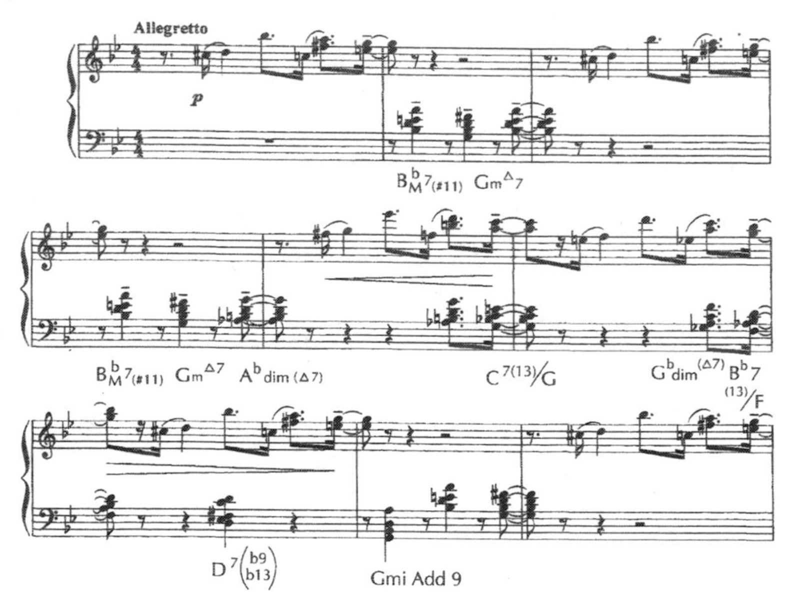

Example 2.107, Myroslav Skoryk, *Caprice*, mm. 1-9

Caprice contains two variations, as listed below in Figure 2.10.

<u>Jazz piece #4, *Caprice*</u>

Var. I: Mm. 34-64
Var. II: Mm. 65-89

Figure 2.10, Variation outline for *Caprice*

In Variation I, Skoryk uses the customary syncopated melodic line with dotted rhythms initiated in the head theme. In place of a walking bass, Skoryk chooses chord ninths (reminiscent of the opening harmonies) in syncopated accompaniment to the melody (see Example 2.108).

Example 2.108, Myroslav Skoryk, *Caprice*, mm. 33-38

The second variation begins with the upbeat to m. 65 and sharply contrasts with the previous material. Skoryk calls this "a theme that recalls a fugue subject with its unexpected rhythmic counterpoint." Oddly, however, this so-called theme and its counterpoint do not function as a fugue.

Example 2.109, Myroslav Skoryk, *Caprice*, mm. 64-70

More important is the fact that within Variation II, the texture and figuration beginning in m. 80 change radically to an unaccented syncopated and repetitive eighth-note—eighth-rest pattern, marked *piano subito*. The right hand uses double thirds, followed by double fourths and octave-with-fifth chords which lead to the climactic arrival of the dominant stated as C#/D octave notes (mm. 88-89). Skoryk notes, "The repeated C#/D pitches bring the variation to a close using the first two notes of the main theme which is restated beginning in m. 90" (see Example 2.110).

Example 2.110, Myroslav Skoryk, *Caprice*, mm. 79-91

Skoryk states that the theme of the fifth piece, *In an Old Jazz Style*, is "intentionally related to a typical jazz theme from the 1930s [big band and swing] jazz period." In describing the typical features of 1930s jazz themes, Gridley writes:

> Sometimes, portions within the passages were passed back and forth, so that it sounded as though one section of the band posed a question and another section answered it. This technique, also common in other forms and eras of world music, is called question and answer, call and response, or responsorial style . . . short, simple phrases called riffs were used by some big bands as essential elements of their style. At times, different riffs were assigned to various sections of the band and played against each other (Gridley p. 89).

In this way, Skoryk emulates the big band swing style in the melody line, answered by the inner voices of the right hand. Another simultaneous and equally important feature of this opening is the stride/walking bass, which is also a common figuration in 1930s jazz style. Example 2.111 shows the first eight measures (head) of this thirty-two bar song form while Figure 2.11 outlines each variation by measure number (see Example 2.111).

Example 2.111, Myroslav Skoryk, *In an Old Jazz Style*, mm. 1-8

<u>Jazz piece #5, *In an Old Jazz Style*</u>

Var. I: Mm. 33-54
Var. II: Mm.65-96
Var. III: Mm. 97-end

Figure 2.11, Variation outline for *In an Old Jazz Style*

Beginning in m. 33, Variation I continues the opening theme's general feel but features triplet rhythms (which create a feel of "swinging") in both the left and right-hand parts and melodic ornamentation in the melody (see Example 2.112).

Example 2.112, Myroslav Skoryk, *In an Old Jazz Style*, mm. 33-39

Variation 11 (mm. 65ff) features right-hand syncopated seventh and ninth chords answered by the left-hand sixteenth and dotted eighth-note rhythm. Measures 71-72 give way to a walking bass line, abruptly leading back to this variation's opening figuration in m. 73 (see Example 2.113).

Example 2.113, Myroslav Skoryk, *In an Old Jazz Style*, mm. 65-73

Beginning in m. 97, the last variation is dominated by the octave-with-fifth texture over a steady "on-the-beat" seventh chord accompaniment in the left hand. Skoryk chose this accompaniment to imitate the textural style of Erroll Garner who utilized this figuration heavily in his piano playing. Gridley confirms this and writes: "Several aspects of Garner's approach have assumed trademark quality for his name. One is that his left hand played a chord on each beat as a rhythm guitarist might" (Gridley p. 102) (see Example 2.114).

Example 2.114, Myroslav Skoryk, *In an Old Jazz Style*, mm. 97-101

In addition, Skoryk employs another of Garner's stylistic hallmarks: the unexpected accentuation of harmony from the first beat to the fourth beat beginning at m. 113 (see Example 2.115). Skoryk refers to this as "a sudden maneuvering in which I was influenced by the typical style and spirit of Erroll Garner."

Example 2.115, Myroslav Skoryk, *In an Old Jazz Style*, mm. 113-116

Typical with many of his works, the ending of this piece contains an improvisatory recitative passage. Skoryk says, "This brings to mind a comparison and influence from Chopin's *Prelude* in F Major." The last measure of the piece contains an F major 7th chord superimposed with a G#m7th which spells a near octatonic scale (in jazz, a diminished scale) (see Example 2.116). Perhaps the G#m7th originates from the opening G# melody note.

Example 2.116, Myroslav Skoryk, *In an Old Jazz Style*, mm. 125-6

Example 2.117, Frederic Chopin, *Prelude, op. 28 No. 23* mm. 20-22

In titling the last piece in this cycle *Arabesque*, Skoryk seems to imply a connection with French musical impressionism. For example, parallel seventh chords strongly reminiscent of Debussy accompany the main theme. In discussing this opening, however, Skoryk avoids mention of Debussy, saying, "My intention is to utilize the seventh chord, a staple in jazz style, varying its role by way of melodic and harmonic exchange." Interestingly, while this piece is in D minor, the opening begins on a iv7 and later implies tonic by its dominant, but avoids the tonic itself until m. 17 which initiates the bridge. Seventh chords in the left hand in a rich homophonic texture accompany the entire theme (see Examples 2.118 and 2.119). Figure 2.12, shows each variation's occurrence in *Arabesque*.

Example 2.118, Myroslav Skoryk, *Arabesque*, mm. 1-8

Example 2.119, Myroslav Skoryk, *Arabesque*, mm. 17-20

<u>Jazz piece #6, *Arabesque*</u>

Var. I: Mm. 33-64
Var. II: Mm. 65-96
Var. III: Mm. 97-128

Figure 2.12, Variation outline for *Arabesque*

The first variation continues the same texture as the opening but now the left hand accompanies the melody with steady downbeat sevenths (see Example 2.120).

Example 2.120, Myroslav Skoryk, *Arabesque*, mm. 33-36

Variation II (m. 65) utilizes harmonic/melodic exchange with the parallel seventh chords transferred to the right hand, first in block chords (mm. 65-72), then changing figuration to broken sevenths in m. 73. Here, melodic exchange occurs with the melodic development running in the left hand.

Example 2.121, Myroslav Skoryk, *Arabesque*, mm. 65-75

The last variation begins in m. 97 and effectively incorporates pure chordal texture, a technique used by Erroll Garner, about which Gridley writes: "Some of Garner's playing is richly orchestral, and it is harmonically like music of Claude Debussy and Maurice Ravel, a style called French Impressionism. Garner often voiced his melodies chordally instead of letting melody notes sound alone. This has led jazz historian Harvey Pekar to feel that Garner's historical impact may have been to get pianists to think more in terms of chordal playing" (Gridley p. 102).

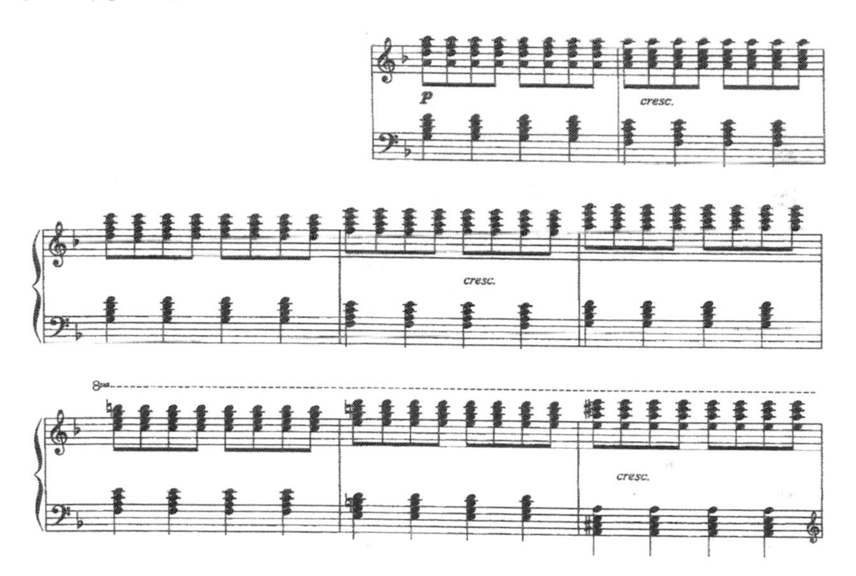

Example 2.122, Myroslav Skoryk, *Arabesque*, mm. 97-101

The composer's attempt in these pieces is to bring the jazz improvisation genre closer to "serious" music. Looking back over this set, Skoryk's creativity comes to the fore in how he plays with the conventional thirty-two bar song form and varies the distribution of melodic, harmonic, and textural material adding to the uniqueness of each piece. Skoryk states, "These jazz pieces are intended for performance by concert pianists as well as music students in colleges and universities." In this respect, Skoryk's cycle is valuable and occupies a unique place in the solo piano repertoire.

Paraphrase on themes of Puccini's opera "Madame Butterfly" (1992)

This piece continues the trend of similar transcriptions by Franz Liszt and recalls the paraphrase style by Vladimir Horowitz. Interestingly, this paraphrase is most likely the first such effort with this opera. Within this virtuosic piece Skoryk incorporates several types of piano techniques. These include brilliant passagework, chordal passages, a toccata-style exposition, and cantilena melodies, which are typical of the music in this opera.

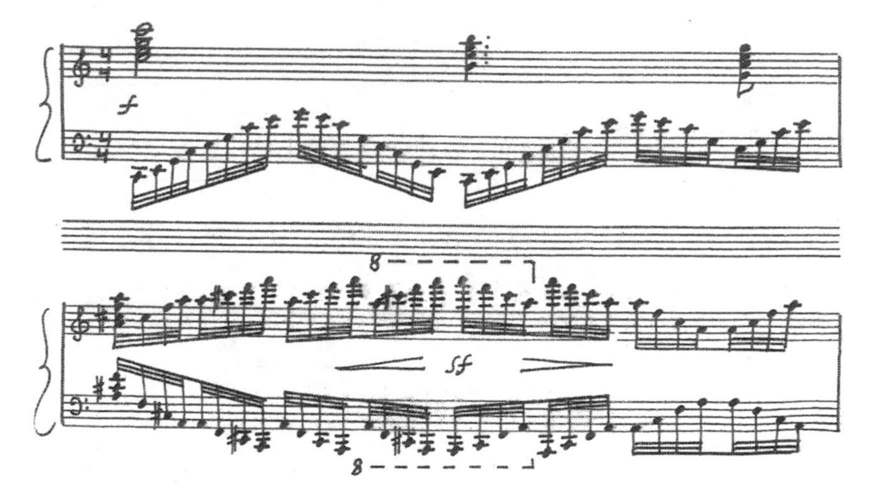

Example 2.123, Myroslav Skoryk, *Paraphrase on themes from Puccini's opera Madame Butterfly,* Virtuosic passage, mm. 136-137

Example 2.124, Myroslav Skoryk, *Paraphrase on themes from Puccini's opera Madame Butterfly*, Virtuosic passage, mm. 142-143

This eight-minute piece is constructed in a dramatic manner, condensing the entire plot of the opera by using the music's most effective melodies and setting them in a virtuosic framework. For the most part, these melodies utilize thematic material played by the orchestra, and themes and/or arias sung by the character Butterfly. Not surprisingly, Skoryk centers his paraphrase on Butterfly, the role his great aunt sang. The music portrays the young Japanese girl and her unfortunate love and tragic death. In general, Skoryk retains the harmonic language of the opera in his paraphrase. Perhaps only at the beginning and end do we find an unexpected juxtaposition of G-flat major followed by an E-minor chord, the latter harshly dissonant against the continuing melodic figuration in G-flat.

Example 2.125, Myroslav Skoryk, *Paraphrase on themes from Puccini's opera Madame Butterfly*, mm. 1-2

Appropriately, the work closes with a direct quote of the opera's most famous tune, the soprano aria, "Un bel di, vedremo."

Example 2.126, Myroslav Skoryk, *Paraphrase on themes from Puccini's opera Madame Butterfly*, mm. 147-154

The chart below (see Figure 2.13) summarizes the opera's themes, arias, characters, and their precise occurrences as they appear in Skoryk's paraphrase and the piano/vocal score of the opera (Dover edition, see bibliography).

Aria/Theme Character(s)	**Plot and Piano/Vocal score page location**	**Skoryk's Paraphrase location in score**
Duet (Butterfly/Pinkerton) "É un po'dura" "Se viè caro sul momento"	(Act. I)—Butterfly/Pinkerton - p. 44-45: Butterfly introduces Pinkerton to friends. This theme is later heard in Butterfly's Aria p. 82-84	Mm. 5-9
Aria (Butterfly) "D'amor venni alle soglie"	(Act I)—Butterfly, expressing happiness and love for Pinkerton just prior to meeting Pinkerton with her friend's p. 39	Mm. 10-22
Prelude-(Orchestra)	(Act I)—Opening of opera Prelude theme, p. 1-5	Mm. 23-50 (exact quote in mm. 35-36)
Orchestral material (Bonze/Pinkerton) and others "Cio-cio-san!"	(Act I)—Butterfly's uncle Bonze (and family) are angry at her renouncing her true religion and plans to wed p. 97-102	Mm. 51-112
Duet (Butterfly/Suzuki) "Pigri ed obesi son gli Dei Giapponesi"	(Act II)—Butterfly/Suzuki await return of Pinkerton p. 136-140	Mm. 113-134
Aria (Butterfly) "Ancora un passo or via"	(Act I)—Butterfly sings of happiness as climbing to summit with Sharpless and friends p. 36-38	Mm. 136-146
Aria (Butterfly) "Un bel dì vedremo"	(Act II)—Butterfly sings of being reunited with Pinkerton as his ship sails into port. This is the opera's most famous aria p. 146-150	Mm. 147-154
Aria (Butterfly) "Amore, addio!"	(Act II, Part 2)—Butterfly's lament and death by self inflicted dagger wound to chest p. 278	Mm. 154-160 (and 161-171)

Figure 2.13, Thematic outline chart for Myroslav Skoryk's, *Paraphrase on themes from Puccini's opera Madame Butterfly*

Melody for Piano (1994)

This little piece in small ternary form is the last work for piano Skoryk has written to date. It was originally written for the movie “Vysokyi pereval”–(“*The High Mountain Pass*”), which premiered in Ukraine in the 1980s. Since that time *Melody* became very popular in Ukraine and beyond her borders. It exists in many variants: for violin and piano, violoncello and piano, for orchestra, string quartet and piano trio. It was through popular demand that Skoryk made an arrangement for piano solo. *Melody* combines what Skoryk states as “characteristic features of Ukrainian folklore” along with individual features of the composer’s style.

The opening phrase, mm.1-8, divides into 2 + 2 + 4, ending in a half cadence. The meter is interesting: the 4/4 time signature is changed to 3/4 in m. 4, about which Skoryk says, “This rhythmic change creates a unified statement.” Skoryk describes the tonal plan as follows: “The opening phrase, by repeating itself, reaches the high note A in m. 3 and then fluently descends and modulates from A minor to C major ending in a half cadence in A minor in m. 8 (E maj = V/A minor returning in m. 9). This tonal plan: A minor, C major, E major originates out of Ukrainian songs and *Melody* is bound with folk melos intonations.” Skoryk continues, “after studying dozens upon dozens of Ukrainian folk songs, I recognized the precise melodic theme’s form and took this as my model.”

Example 2.127, Myroslav Skoryk, *Melody*, mm. 1-8

Measure 9-16 repeats the opening phrase, adding a melodic counterpoint in the tenor left-hand part.

Example 2.128, Myroslav Skoryk, *Melody*, mm. 9-16

Beginning at m. 17 the short development consists of a modulatory sequence aided by the ascending bass line. The melody passes from C-sharp minor to G-sharp minor (m. 20), then from B minor to F-sharp (m. 23) and finally arrives at the dominant of A minor at m. 24. This gradual movement upward in two waves culminates in the reprise in m. 25.

Example 2.129, Myroslav Skoryk, *Melody*, Dev. and Recap. mm. 17-26

The reprise at m. 25 is enriched with additional voices, and the first four notes of the main theme motive are imitated in the accompaniment. This work has proven to be the most popular among all Skoryk's works. It is well known that in Ukraine it can be heard almost daily in concert halls, on radio, and television. It is akin to the popularity and recognition of American composer Samuel Barber's *Adagio for Strings*. A recent performance of *Melody* was heard during the inaugural concert for Ukrainian President Viktor Yushchenko in Kiev, January 23, 2005.

Chapter 3

Case Study of the *Burlesque* (1963)

For Skoryk, the 1963 *Burlesque* begins the sharp ascent towards full maturity. The *Burlesque* is a charming work and perhaps the most popular piano piece from Skoryk's output. Its immediate energy and primordial force thrills and startles the listener. It is evident that none of Skoryk's works from this period contain such a variety of stylistic features. Kyianovska says, "In this first period of Skoryk's compositions are few works where the accuracy of combining diverse stylistic features in one larger work is achieved with master precision" (Kyianovska p. 42). Skoryk chose to write this piece with a focus on the virtuosic element but also with what he calls "an ironic tone." The overall form of this composition is clear: Skoryk utilizes the sonata-rondo form, i.e.,

Refrain 1	Episode 1	Refrain 2	Episode 2	Refrain 3	Episode 1	Refrain 4
		(Partial)		(Partial)	(transposed)	(Partial/coda)
A	B	A	C	A	B	A

In his book, *Classical Form,* William Caplin summarizes the constituent parts of this form: "As its label suggests, the sonata-rondo combines features of the five-part rondo (with its regular alternation of refrains and couplets [episodes] and the sonata (with its tripartite organization of exposition, development, and recapitulation) (Caplin p. 235).

The pyramid diagram below (Figure 3.1) outlines the design of the sonata-rondo in arch format as applied to the *Burlesque*. The first pyramid shows the thematic outline which corresponds to the form noted above while the second pyramid illustrates the tonal scheme with the main key (pitch) centers used.

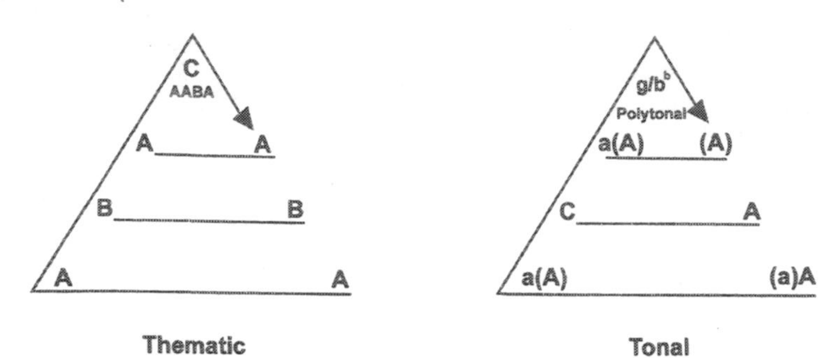

Figure 3.1, Thematic and Tonal Outline of the *Burlesque*

The *Burlesque's* thematic material consists of a variety of figurative and stylistic elements which can be traced along the crossroads of historic traditions. The main motive reminds one of the duple-meter Ukrainian Carpathian Dance, which Kyianovska confirms: "Without a doubt, the beginning motive is innate with the [Ukrainian] Kolomyika reminding the listener of the temperamental violinists of the Hutsul [Hutsul peoples in Ukrainian Carpathia] land" (Kyia-novska p. 43). However, the syncopated accompaniment and frequent changes in the main theme's accentuation bring it closer to jazz and ragtime. In addition, the agitated repetition of the motive, which returns to the beginning note B-flat, incites what Skoryk calls "a strain of rhythmic pulsation suggesting a toccata analogous to Prokofiev's *Toccata*." Actually, this almost paradoxical play of styles and influences adds to the sensation of "Burlesquishness" and creates a sense of theatricality throughout this instrumental work.

(Form Chart): formulated by the author as applied to Skoryk's *Burlesque*
sonata-rondo form = A B A C A B A
(AABA)

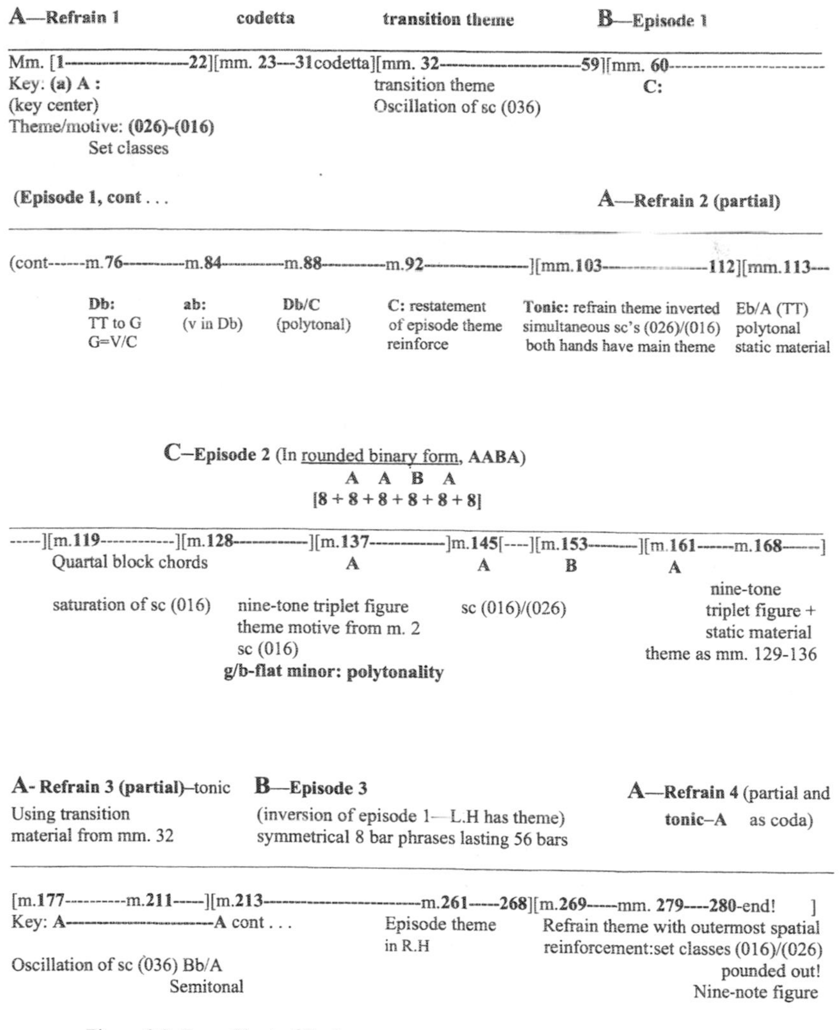

Figure 3.2, Form Chart of Burlesque

Here again, the influence of Bartók is evident in that Skoryk uses the set class (016) as his main intervallic/thematic motive in this work. The *Burlesque* features a variety of sonorities. The intervals of the perfect 4th (interval class 5) as well as the augmented 4th/diminished 5th (interval class 6) saturate much of this work. The reason for this is that the set class (016) contains the interval of the augmented 4th and perfect 4th. In addition, the unstable nature of the set class (016)—whether expressed as m2nd + P4th, P4th + tritone, etc.—contributes to the expression of tonal ambiguity.

Refrain 1 (+ codetta & transition), mm. 1-59.

The first thirteen measures of the refrain contain all the motivic material that Skoryk develops throughout this work. This is less evident in the episode 1 section (its role being one of thematic/rhythmic contrast) although intervallic traces of the opening refrain theme such as set class (026), are embedded in the episode 1 theme beginning at m. 60 (see Example 3.1).

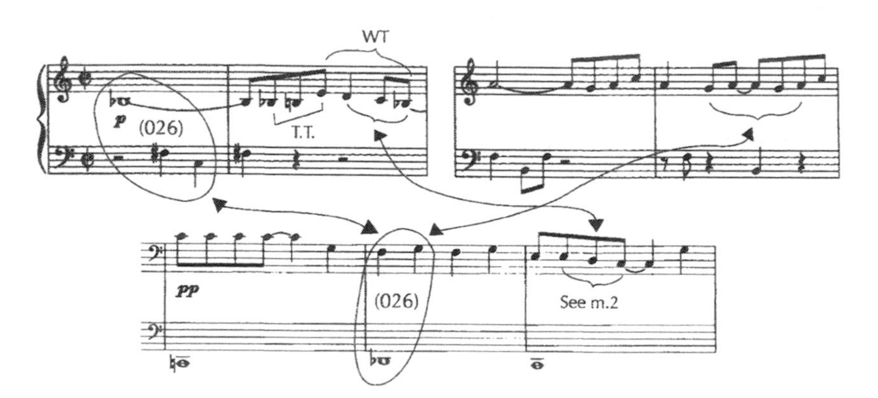

Example 3.1, Myroslav Skoryk: *Burlesque*, mm. 1-2, 7-8, and 60-62

Episode 2 beginning in m. 129 also uses motivic/thematic material from the opening refrain theme in mm. 137-138 (see Example 3.2).

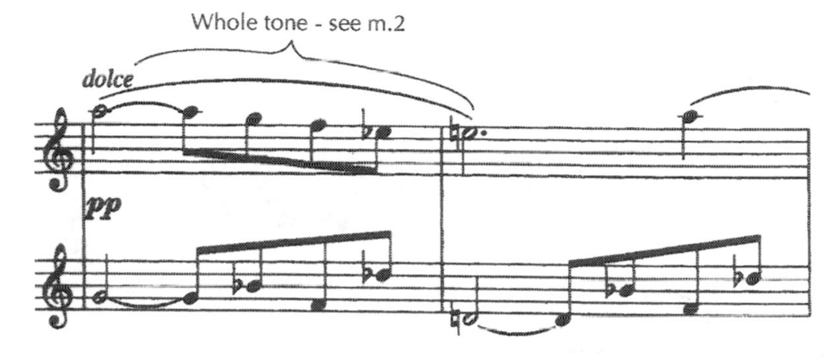

Example 3.2, Myroslav Skoryk: *Burlesque*, mm. 137-138

The refrain 1 section (mm. 1-59) contains an asymmetrical phrase structure 7+7+9+8+10+8+10. The sudden accentuations initiated through the use of *sforzando* chords and jumping from one section to another convey what Skoryk calls "open or implied sarcasm," the illustrative effect portraying "a two-faced mask, where one side is laughter and the other wry. . . . The refrain theme itself has an impulsive nature, directed to overcome any obstacle and almost destroying everything in its path."

The main pitch center in the opening refrain section is A—fluctuating between A Aeolian (A natural minor) and A major—although the main theme's initial statement centers on the pitch B-flat, a semitonal relationship to the pitch A. Measure 1 contains the pitch classes B-flat, F-sharp and C, which taken together represent a member of set class (026). Skoryk utilizes the tonally unstable nature of this pitch-class set (due to the tritone within this set) to transpose the thematic material in the opening fourteen measures. The first three pitch classes in the right hand of m. 2 are B-flat, B-natural, and E. This trichord is a member of set class (016), which also contains a tritone, and as mentioned is the main thematic/intervallic figure used throughout this work. The descending notes of the theme in m. 2 show whole-tone characteristics as displayed in Example 3.2. The right hand-ascent from Bb to E also spans the distance of a tritone. This tritone, Bb to E, implies the pitch E as the dominant scale degree in A, an important relationship throughout the work.

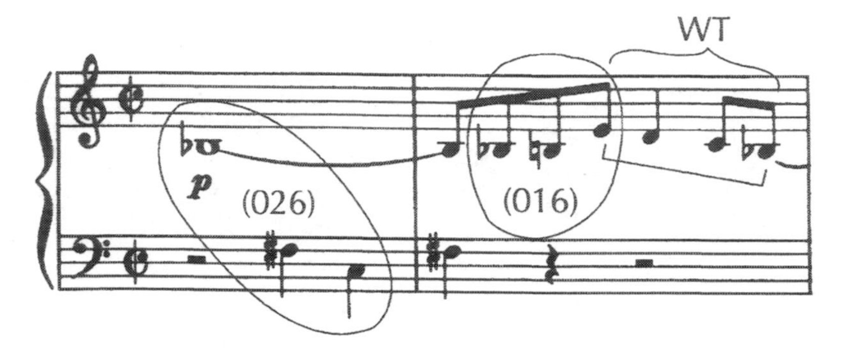

Example 3.3, Myroslav Skoryk: *Burlesque*, mm. 1-2

The transposition of the opening (026) trichord down a semitone in m. 6 (and the set class (016) reaching the note A4 in m. 6) establishes A as a pitch center within the context of A-Aeolian (see Examples 3.3 and 3.4).

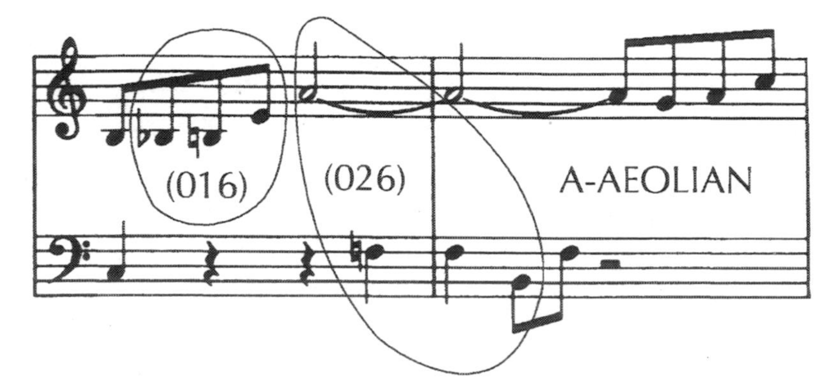

Example 3.4, Myroslav Skoryk: *Burlesque*, mm. 6-7

Furthermore, the prolonged reiteration and circling around A4 (shown with arrows in Example 3.5) in mm. 7-12 firmly establishes A as the main pitch center.

Example 3.5, Myroslav Skoryk: *Burlesque*, mm. 7-12

In mm. 13-14 the transposition of set class (026) down a semitone (from the pitch class set (F, A, B) to interval set class (E, G#, Bb)) leads to a G# (and the set class (016)) in the right hand, which functions like scale degree 7 (the leading tone) of A. To summarize, in mm. 1-14 Skoryk maneuvers around the pitch A4 in the right hand as the music descends through a series of (026) trichords (see Example 3.6 below).

Example 3.6, Myroslav Skoryk: *Burlesque*, mm. 1-14

In measures 14-18 the set class (016) is projected with sharp syncopated accents leading to the cadential passage in m. 19. Measures 19-22 re-establish the pitch center A by emphasizing its tonic triadic pitch members A, E and C# along with reiterating the set classes (026) and (016) in mm. 20-22, thereby implying a tonic cadence. Regarding the refrain theme's close, Caplin says, "Much of what we observed in connection with the main theme of the five-part rondo holds for the sonata-rondo as well, especially the requirement that the theme close with a perfect authentic cadence" (Caplin p. 237).

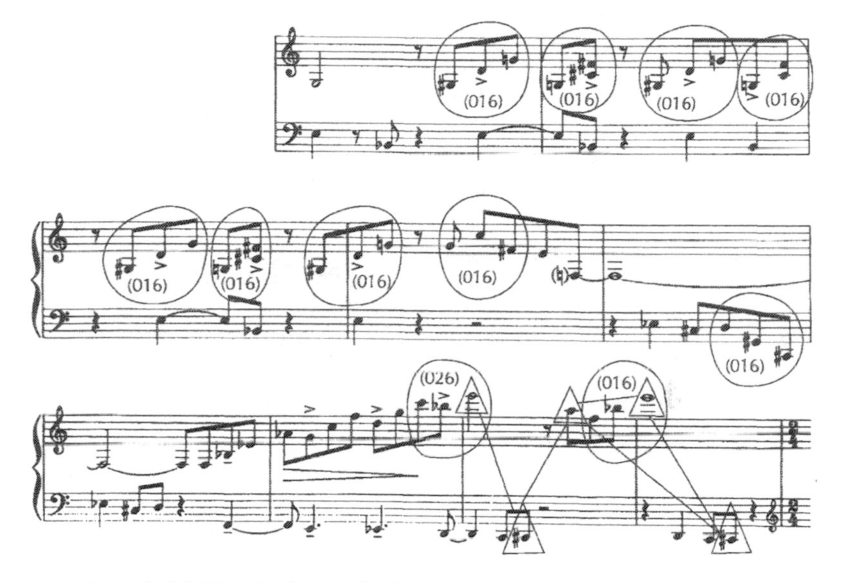

Example 3.7, Myroslav Skoryk: *Burlesque*, mm. 14-22

The thematic material of this codetta theme in the right hand part of m. 24 (see Example 3.9) is derived from the melodic material in m. 2 as shown in Example 3.8.

Example 3.8, Myroslav Skoryk: *Burlesque*, m. 2

Example 3.9, Myroslav Skoryk: *Burlesque*, mm. 23-31

In addition to emphasizing the pitch center A, mm. 23-31 begin and end with the set class (016) and function as a codetta theme concluding the first part of the refrain. Measure 31 comes to rest on the Eb/Bb dyad. The tritone (beginning with A4 in m. 28 and coming to rest on Eb4 in m. 31) is further emphasized by the interval Eb-A (A being the refrain pitch center), as well as Bb-E, where E represents the dominant of A. (See Example 3.9.)

Beginning with the anacrusis (m. 31), the transition material in the right hand (set class (016)) to m. 32 uses the same trichord in the left hand as m. 2 (Bb, B-natural, and E). This is supported by an oscillating trichord accompaniment of two transpositions of set class (036), the diminished triad. The first (036) trichord containing the notes B, D, F implies vii° in C, while the other, C, E-flat, F# implies vii° of D-flat, a reference to the semitonal C/D-flat relationship that subsequently dominates in episode 1. Another way to look at this passage is that the pitches (B, D, F) = vii°/C and the (F#, [A], C, Eb) = vii°7/G which =

vii°7/V/C—the pitch D5 resolves the appoggiatura E5 (see mm. 33, 37, 38, 40-41). Thus the diminished chords oscillate between the dominant of C and the V/V of C. This ten-measure phrase (mm. 32-41) emphasizes the main pitch center A by a recurring emphasis on the notes A, C, and E as shown by the arrows in Example 3.10.

Example 3.10, Myroslav Skoryk: *Burlesque*, mm. 31-41

Measures 42 and 43 contain the same three-note motive used in m. 13. Another sudden shift in m. 43 forms set class (026) and affirms the pitch A3 (which is sustained for two measures) in m. 44 as shown in Example 3.11.

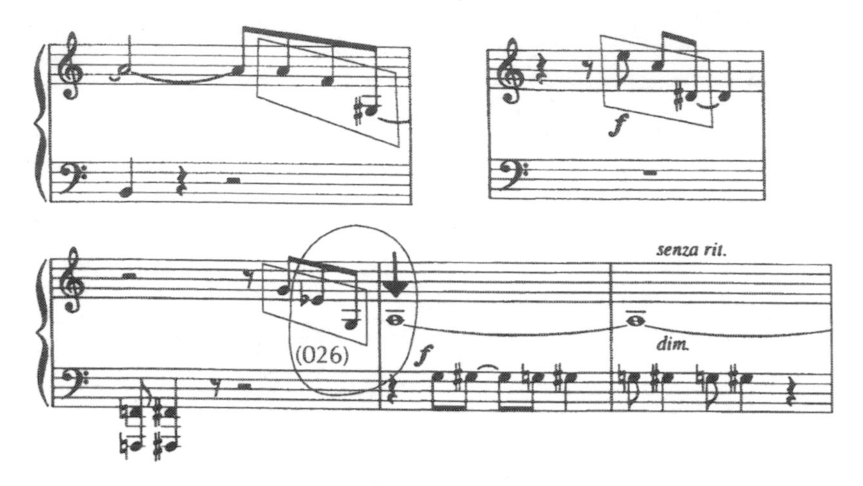

Example 3.11, Myroslav Skoryk: *Burlesque*, mm. 13, 42, and 43-45

In this work we encounter a modern construction of modal tonality and harmonic organization. Notwithstanding the complicated modal and tonal displacement or, as Skoryk says, "shifting of twelve-tone diatonic modes," Skoryk avoids dodecaphonic technique totally. Indeed, we sense the main tonal center of the refrain on the note A in the cadence at mm. 47-49 as shown in Example 3.12. This culmination is achieved by the repeated emphasis of the pitch A as discussed thus far.

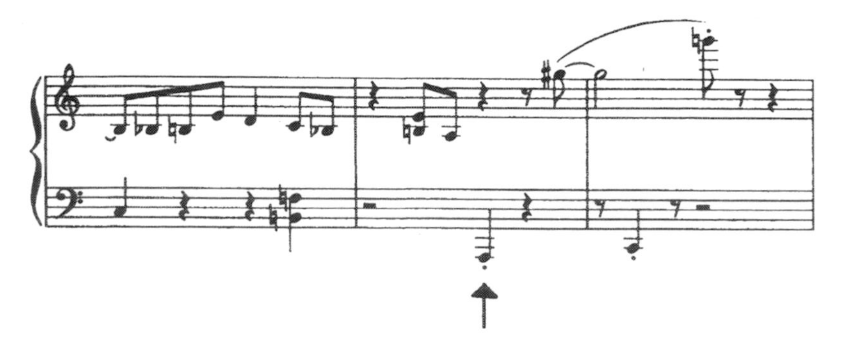

Example 3.12, Myroslav Skoryk: *Burlesque*, mm. 47-49

Measures 50 to 59 conclude the refrain section with the reiterated accented notes C# and C-natural (starting in m. 54) and the accented pitch A2 in mm. 55-57. The C-sharp also functions as the third scale degree in A (enharmonically equivalent to Db). However, it is C-natural that finally wins this battle between pitches that conveniently leads to episode 1 (section B) at m. 60, now in the key center of C (the relative of A minor). Another way to look at this cadential section is the so-called quasi "dominant lock" which is set up by the tritone relationship mentioned; from this perspective, C# represents a tritone substitute for G, the dominant of C (see Example 3.13).

Example 3.13, Myroslav Skoryk: *Burlesque*, mm. 50-62

Episode 1, mm. 60-102.

The key scheme found in a typical classical rondo form shows the first digression, in this case episode 1, as being either in the dominant or relative key. The *Burlesque's* refrain pitch center was A (minor); logically, then, Skoryk implies the relative motion by a move to C in episode 1. As is typically seen in rondo forms, the first episode or digression following the refrain section contains a new theme. While the episode's role is one of contrast to the refrain theme, they may be motivically or intervalically related to one another, sometimes in a highly disguised manner.

Here, a small motivic and intervallic link between the episode and refrain theme is evident (including the set class (026) in m. 61) when comparing them (see Example 3.1, comparing mm. 1-2 & 60-62). A more significant relationship between the refrain and episode 1 material is the semitone relationship mentioned earlier. In analyzing the refrain, the transposition of set class (026) by semitone was revealed and discussed. As seen in the Example 3.13, the last measures of the refrain section (mm. 58-59) show the reiterated C#/C-natural dyad (interval class 1) with the battle eventually won by the pitch class C-natural at m. 60.

Regarding the phrase structure of the episode 1 theme, a more symmetrical pattern occurs when compared with the somewhat disjointed phrase structure of the refrain section. Figure 3.3 shows the phrase structure for the entire episode 1:

(A A B B A)
[8 + 8 + 8 + 8 + 11]
Mm. 60-----68-----76------84-------92-102

Figure 3.3, Phrase Structure; Myroslav Skoryk: *Burlesque*, mm. 60-102

The last phrase, with the extension of three measures (mm. 100-102), provides a kind of syncopated echo to mm. 98-99 (to be addressed below). Measure 60 begins the first eight-measure phrase and m. 61 contains the set class (026) with the note Db2. This semitone relationship between C/D-flat foreshadows the modulation to D-flat in m. 76 and shows the tritone relationship between Db and G—G/V/C.

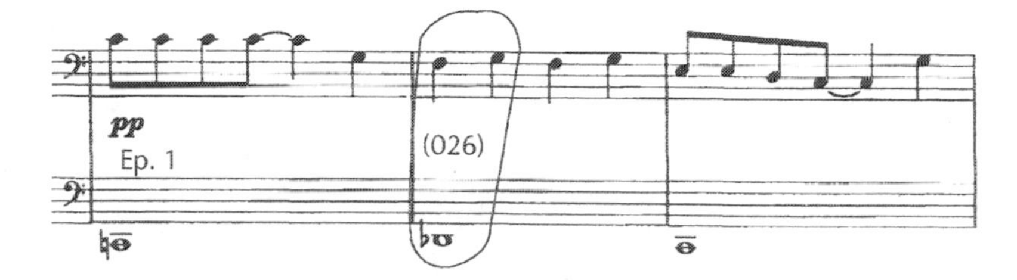

Example 3.14, Myroslav Skoryk: *Burlesque*, mm. 60-62

The following eight measures (mm. 68-75) are a repeat of the episode theme with the addition of a more syncopated and active left-hand counterpoint. This left-hand material accentuates the pitch D-flat. Skoryk uses the C/D-flat semitone relationship to effect a modulation from the pitch center C to D-flat in m. 76. This is effectively set up by the chromatic arrival in the left hand in mm. 74-75 which provides dissonant support for the right hand scale in m. 75, and the simultaneous Ab1 and Db4 on beat 4 strongly imply V7/Db (see Example 3.15).

Example 3.15, Myroslav Skoryk: *Burlesque*, mm. 68-75

Measures 76-91 contain the overlapping of set classes (016) and (026) and virtuosic double thirds which begin a gradual textural reinforcement. A shift to A-flat minor (v of Db) occurs in m. 84 and again contains the overlapping of the same set classes (see Example 3.16).

Example 3.16, Myroslav Skoryk: *Burlesque*, mm. 76-86

The key center of A-flat minor continues until the recurrence of D-flat in m. 88 (L.H.) leading to a definitive polytonal Db/C statement in the left and right hands in m. 91. This polytonal passage utilizes the D-flat/C-natural semitonal relationship first seen in m. 54 (enharmonically equivalent to C#/C) and thereby prepares the return to the main episode 1 theme in C at m. 92. This instance of polytonality precedes its utilization in episode 2. Measure 92 culminates the textural reinforcement by way of spatial, textural (octave with fifth), and dynamic reinforcement as shown in Example 3.17.

Example 3.17, Myroslav Skoryk: *Burlesque*, mm. 88-102

Refrain 2, mm. 103-127

The restatement of the refrain theme at m. 103 (Example 3.18) contains some new textural additions. First, the upper and lower voices have been inverted; the right-hand melody from m. 1 moves to the bass, and the left hand's F# and C-natural are now found in the high treble register and harmonized with quartal chords. These quartal chords "3x4 on G" form the set class (016) along with the simultaneous use of set class (026) by way of the B-flat, C-natural and F-sharp within m. 103. Second, these two set classes first stated in mm. 1-2 saturate this restatement of the refrain and are intertwined in m. 103. Lastly, the entire restatement of the refrain section (mm. 103-127) shows the main theme emphatically stated by means of large register shifts and sharp accentuation all within an elevated dynamic level. The main refrain theme is now played with both hands throughout and in rhythmic augmentation.

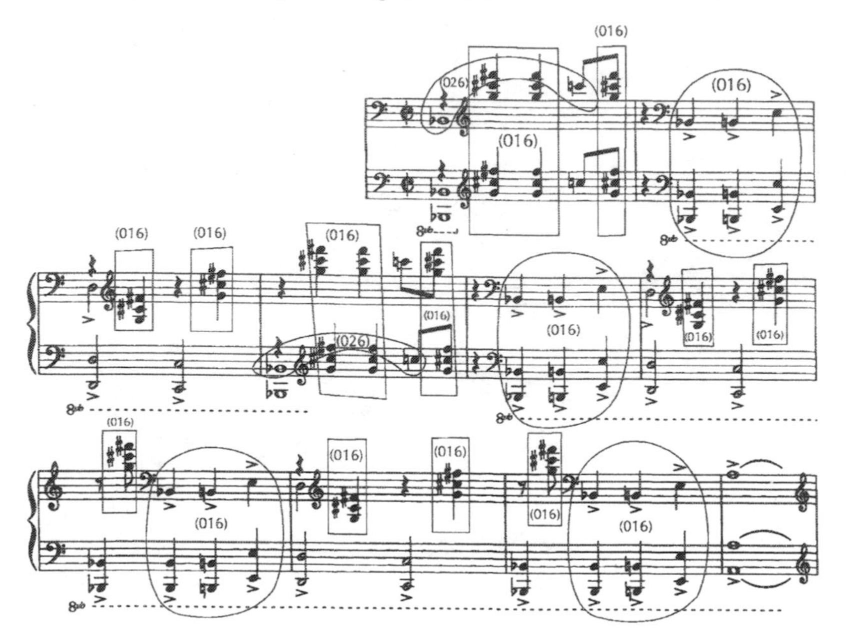

Example 3.18, Myroslav Skoryk: *Burlesque*, mm. 103-112

Measures 113-118 contain a static polytonal passage utilizing the original refrain melodic material between mm. 7-13 (in the R.H.) with the E-flat minor sonority, a tritone distance from A, found in the left hand (see Example 3.19, it also represents an octatonic subset). The prominent pitches Gb/A (which form an augmented 2nd) function as leading tones, which imply the keys G/B-flat minor respectively in the polytonal episode 2 section:

Gb = 7/G minor (enharmonically F#)

A = 7/B-flat minor polytonal set up to m. 129

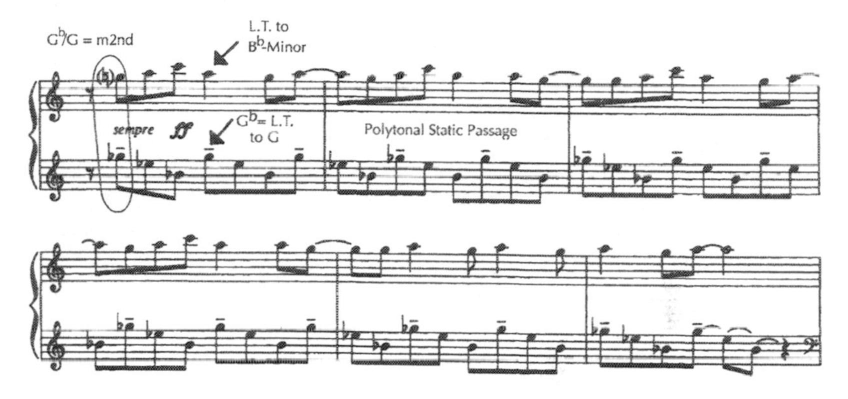

Example 3.19, Myroslav Skoryk: *Burlesque*, mm. 113-118

Measures 119-120 harmonize the exact melodic material first seen in mm. 13-14 (see Example 3.6) now in rhythmic augmentation and with the quartal blocked chords "4x4 on F," "4x4 on D," "4x4 on E," "4x4 on C#" and "4x4 on G." The remaining measures 121-127 continue the opening refrain melodic material, and are again saturated with the signature set class (016) sonority, which concludes the episode 1 section leading to the triplet figure in m. 128 (see Example 3.20).

Example 3.20, Myroslav Skoryk: *Burlesque*, mm. 119-128

Episode 2, mm. 128-176.

The second episode section (mm. 128-176) is in rounded binary form (see Figure 3.4). As with the development section in sonata form, the second episode in sonata-rondo form can either take on a developmental role or provide new material. Skoryk chooses to use a related theme (R.H.) but changes the character and tempo (Andante) in this central section. The phrase structure of this episode yields the symmetrical pattern of six eight-measure phrases, the first and last phrases (mm. 129-136 and mm. 169-176) constituting the static introductory and closing material.

Static intro passage A A B A Static concluding passage

(1) + 8 + 8 + 8 + 8 + 8 + (1) + 8

Nine note Figure ... Nine note Figure

Mm. 128------129------137------145------153------161------168------169------176

Figure 3.4, Myroslav Skoryk: *Burlesque*, mm. 128-176

Significantly, the nine-note figure in m. 128 marked *meno mosso* (see Example 3.20) opens the episode 2 section and returns to close it in m. 168. This melodic figure illustrates what Skoryk termed the "wry [crooked]" side of the mask mentioned earlier. The last triplet in m. 128, containing the pitches Bb, F, Db, spells a B-flat minor triad (continuing in m. 129-136) and the G-D in the left hand (mm. 129-136) a G-minor triad (Bb is the "common tone"). This Bb is a minor 2nd above A and a tritone from E—the dominant of A, the expected key center of the upcoming restatement of the refrain section (see Example 3.21 below).

Example 3.21, Myroslav Skoryk*: Burlesque*, mm. 129-136

Measures 129-136 begin the static polytonal passage between G-minor and B-flat minor, the left hand taking over the right-hand material in m. 136 and setting up the entrance of the right-hand theme in m. 137. This melodic (R.H.)

material in m. 137 directly corresponds to the closing theme of the first refrain (m. 24), which initially comes from m. 2 (see Example 3.22 below).

Example 3.22, Myroslav Skoryk: *Burlesque*, mm. 2, 24, 136-138

Example 3.23 below shows the next two eight-measure phrases (mm. 137-152) with the statement of the episode 2 main theme. Set class (016) is used at the end of each phrase in this section in a cadential manner (mm. 144, 151-152).

Example 3.23, Myroslav Skoryk: *Burlesque*, mm. 136-152

The central (B) section of episode 2 beginning in m. 153 (marked *stringendo*) contains the fusion of set classes (016) and (026) oscillating around the pitch C#. This central section of episode 2 begins to recall the character of the refrain section. Kyianovska writes, "The central part of the [second] episode shows the grotesque dance trying to burst through [this lyrical episode] with its sharpness, its first attempt [mm. 153-154] not succeeding but with every next repetition becomes bolder and stronger [dynamically] only to wither away" (Kyianovska p. 44). This withering away leads to a restatement of the main theme, moving in turn to the nine-note figure previously mentioned which initiates the return of the static eight-measure passage introducing episode 2 (see Example 3.24). Skoryk says, "This passage of nine tones, like its first statement in m. 168, acts as an illusion of the lyrical theme."

Example 3.24, Myroslav Skoryk: *Burlesque*, mm. 150-170

Regarding the episode 2 section, Kyianovska describes its illustrative effect as "a slowly passing lyrical island, and the only manifestation of human feeling within this burlesque, transparent—a gentle tune twinkling as an unreachable distant light" (Kyianovska p. 43). In my interviews with Skoryk, the composer summed up this central section (episode 2) as "human feeling with a delicate and transparent tune twinkling as a phantom aureole, distant and unreachable."

Refrain 3, mm. 177-212.

The reprise or part three (refrain, episode, refrain) of the *Burlesque,* beginning with the Tempo I in m. 177, is abbreviated with respect to the first (part 1) ABA section. More specifically, the refrain following episode 2 does not begin with a recapitulation of the initial refrain theme as in m. 1, but with the identical transition theme first used in m. 32 (see Example 3.10 and 3.25). Caplin describes this deviation: "At this point, the complete structure of the rondo refrain is usually brought back . . . but like any return, an abridged or incomplete version may appear instead" (Caplin p. 239).

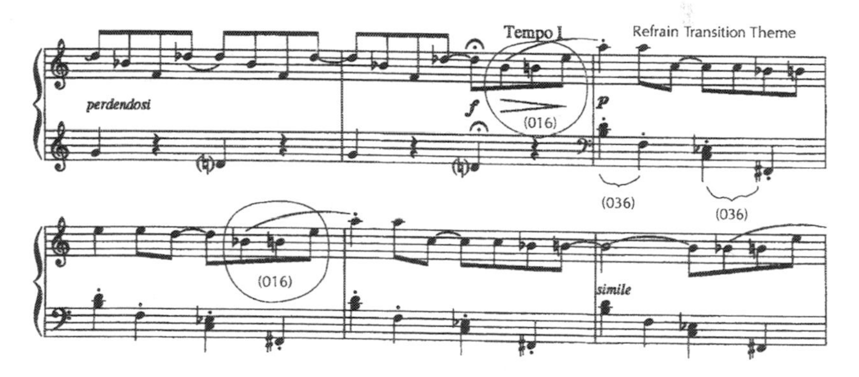

Example 3.25, Myroslav Skoryk: *Burlesque*, 175-180

Skoryk intensifies the section through spatial and dynamic reinforcement, shifting between B-flat and B-natural (the L.H set class (036)) at mm. 177, 191,

201 and finally reaching the Bb/A semitonal reiteration (octave-fifth chords) in mm. 211-212) (see Example 3.26). In this way Skoryk utilizes the semitone relationship precisely as used in the C-sharp/C-natural "dominant lock" at m. 59 (see Example 3.13), thereby leading back to the episode 3 section (m. 213) now in its customary tonic pitch center A (see Example 3.26 below).

Example 3.26, Myroslav Skoryk: *Burlesque*, 191, 201, 211-214

Episode 3, mm. 213-268

Episode 3 shows the composer's creativity in that the theme is now in invertible counterpoint with its statement in the left hand (compare mm. 60ff). Moreover, the theme functions as a repetitive basso ostinato passage in symmetrical eight-measure phrases lasting 56 measures without any key shifts (modulations) as seen in episode 1. It is gradually built up from its initial two-voice texture (in *pianissimo*) by the addition of two, three, and four-note chords jumping between high and middle registers in the right hand (see Example 3.27). In describing this buildup Kyianovska says, "The third episode portrays a fantastic parade of strength—a grotesque carnival mask draws nearer, demonstrating its sinister grin" (Kyianovska p. 44).

Example 3.27, Myroslav Skoryk: *Burlesque*, mm. 213-221, 229-230, 237-238, 245-246, 253-254

An interesting registral and textural exchange occurs again in m. 261 where the episode theme reaches its culmination and is also "flipped," as first appeared in episode 1 (see Example 3.17, m. 92) with the right hand taking the theme (see Example 3.28).

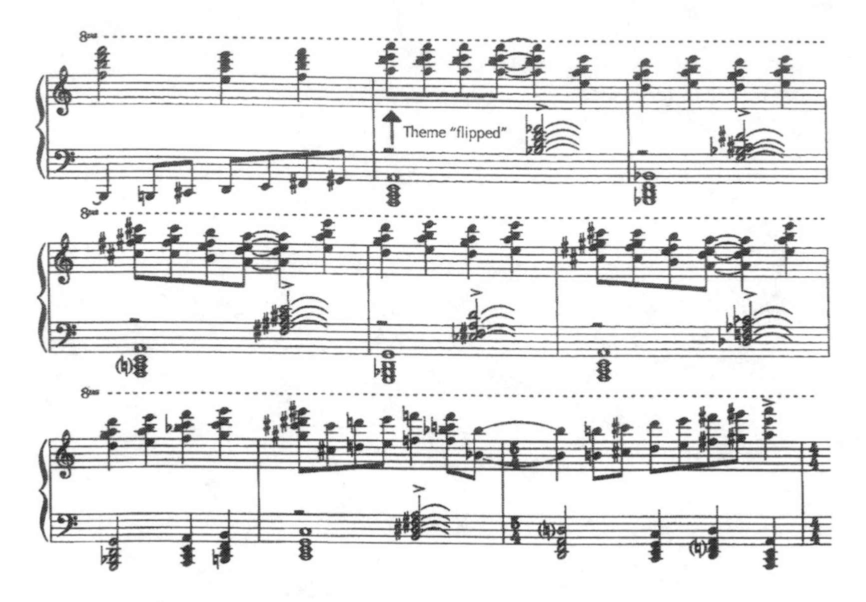

Example 3.28, Myroslav Skoryk: *Burlesque*, mm. 261-268

Refrain 4, mm. 269-end

The *Burlesque's* culmination (in triple *forte*) occurs with the abbreviated re-statement of the refrain theme in m. 269. This final refrain functions as a coda and pounds out the set classes (016) and (026) with its triple *forte* dynamic and virtuosic jumping between the middle and outermost range of the piano. The unexpected ending shows the appearance of the nine-tone figure (m. 279) and ends with the same sonority, set class (026), as m. 1 (see Example 3.29).

Example 3.29, Myroslav Skoryk: *Burlesque*, mm. 269-280

In describing the restatement of the nine-tone figure, Skoryk referred to it as "a kind of confirmation to the unreal passing collision of irony and a crooked smile." It is evident that the *Burlesque* finds the composer entering his period of maturity. In addition to being a required work at the Vladimir Horowitz Piano Competition in Kiev, Ukraine, the *Burlesque* has over the years become Skoryk's most popular piano work.

Chapter 4

Conclusion

Myroslav Skoryk stands at the forefront of contemporary Ukrainian composers for several reasons. First, Skoryk's music is laced with indigenous Ukraine folk music, particularly folk music from the Carpathian Mountain region. His distinctive music transforms modal pitch collections from this region into a modern form of expression, thus creating a unique addition to more recently composed Ukrainian music. Skoryk's first success at incorporating these modes into his early piano cycle *In Carpathian Mountains* (1959) and the *Variations for Piano* (1962) clearly illustrates the impact of this contribution. His cycle of pieces *From the Children's Album* (1966) uses both modal and dance music from the Carpathian region with a clear reference to the duple-meter syncopated Ukrainian dance, the Kolomyika. Based upon Skoryk's aforementioned contributions, it becomes apparent that his first and second stylistic periods, On the Brink of Maturity (1955–1964) and The Wave of New Folklore (1965–1972) feature a general attraction to Ukrainian and American folk music.

Second, Skoryk continues using Ukrainian folk elements and jazz harmonies (from American popular music) and a greater emphasis on syncopated rhythms (also a prominent feature of the Kolomyika as mentioned above). Skoryk's works from this period document the first attempt by a Ukrainian composer to integrate jazz with "serious" music. Prime examples are the *Burlesque* (1963), with its association to jazz and ragtime and the small piano work *Blues* (1963). Moreover, several solo piano works written after this second stylistic period continue to show a marked saturation of jazz elements, including the *Partita No. 5* (1975), the *Toccata* (1978), *Six Preludes and Fugues* (1989), and, most notably, *Six Jazz Pieces* written in 1993. In short, Skoryk must be considered an originator of the utilization and integration of two diverse and distant native music traditions—Ukrainian and American.

Third, Skoryk's use of quotation finds its way into many of his works, thus showing the eclectic mix of different styles within his singular musical language. Skoryk's music utilizes quotation in two ways: thematic cross reference between varying sections of a work; and quoted passages borrowed from different works. The *Partita No. 5* represents the primary example of the composer's use of thematic cross reference from movement to movement, culminating in the finale's direct quotation from all previous movements. The finale also uses "borrowed" quotation; however, the tonal language remains original in spite of its eclectic tendencies. The *Partita No. 5* exemplifies Skoryk's third stylistic period, On the Edge of Neoclassicism (1973–1978), which also includes polystylistic elements and incorporates suggestive hints of music from Bach, Chopin, Rachmaninoff, Liszt, Ravel, and jazz. This trend continues into his next period, In the Labyrinths of Stylish Games (1984–1999). Most noteworthy is his *Six Preludes and Fugues* (1989), which successfully bridges the gap between the baroque style (fugue), jazz, and popular music in a polystylistic way and thus creates, as Skoryk terms this trend, "stylish games."

Skoryk's consistent adherence to standard forms such as sonata, rondo, sonata-rondo, suite, fugue, and theme and variation is verified through the general discussions provided in Chapter 2. A case study of the *Burlesque* (Chapter 3) substantiates Skoryk's structural approach by providing a detailed analysis of a representative solo piano work, revealing his harmonic language (including modal characteristics, semitonal interval game and jazz style), and adherence to the standard formal design, the sonata-rondo.

A complete study of Skoryk's life and music would require several years of historical and musicological research. In the area of biography, however, several facts need to be reexamined in light of Ukraine's intense political situation, including the impact of a stifling Communist atmosphere upon Skoryk's compositional decisions and the deeper meaning of this social setting for his personal and professional life. In meetings with Skoryk, he has alluded only briefly to these influences upon his works. A comprehensive appreciation of the impact of Soviet life and politics as well as twentieth-century music upon Skoryk and his work may be successfully achieved only through added research and interviews with the composer himself.

Researching Skoryk and his oeuvre, however, poses many difficulties since the preponderance of information in both article and book formats is found solely in Eastern Europe, thus necessitating a well-organized examination of various archives throughout the region. In addition, to place Skoryk within the contexts of both the European and American music of our time would require closer examination of Skoryk's contemporaries, along with American jazz.

In conducting this research, the author has provided important and significant new facts regarding Skoryk's life and music (specifically the solo piano works). Through detailed analysis and general commentary, the techniques and source material for his solo piano works are unveiled for the reader. Interviews conducted with the composer have provided valuable insights into his music and his persona. This research project is also the first of its kind to cover the entire span of Skoryk's solo piano works and, in doing so, to provide the first analytical discussion of many of these works.

Significantly, this book also includes a detailed analysis of Skoryk's solo piano works with musical examples referenced within the text. Prior to this book, extant sources have failed to provide musical examples or detailed analyses, offering no more than general commentary on the composer's works, thereby leaving the reader without a viable reference point with which to approach the music itself. This book also provides a complete catalogue of Skoryk's solo piano works to date, including documentation of their availability in the United States, Russia, and Ukraine, thus enabling future researchers to gather necessary scores for further study. Finally, through the author's direct interviews with the composer, this book reveals for the first time Skoryk's reminiscences on how a number of individual experiences, several of which he had never before publicly discussed, have influenced his artistic and personal development.

These interviews with Skoryk have also led to broader insights regarding the composer's views on music as well as the specific sources of inspiration behind his works. Previously unknown details affecting Skoryk's professional and personal decisions are documented as well, thus enhancing understanding of his stylistic development. Skoryk also discusses specific passages from his solo piano works during these interviews, thus illuminating his artistic goals and views regarding his successes and failures. In essence, the Skoryk interviews documented and assessed throughout this book, as well as attendant analyses, present a convincing argument that Myroslav Skoryk is one of the twentieth and twenty-first centuries' distinctive musical voices.

Appendix

Complete list of published and unpublished solo piano works of Myroslav Skoryk

The following list of solo piano works by Myroslav Skoryk is available in the U.S.A. by Duma Music Inc., 557 Barron Avenue, Woodbridge, New Jersey 07095.

Work	Year Published
Album Leaf for piano solo	1999
Blues for piano solo	1997
Burlesque (from the collection "Music without Borders")	1996
From the Children's Album	2001
Melody	1996
Partita No. 5 (in modo retro) for piano solo	2006
Piano Variations	2001
Six Jazz Pieces for piano solo	2003
Toccata	2010

Forthcoming works to be published by Duma Music, Inc.

(by expected date)

Six Preludes and Fugues	2010
Cycle: *In Carpathian Mountains*	2010

The following works are in manuscript form and in the private collection of the author

Paraphrase on opera themes of Giacomo Puccini's Madame Butterfly
Prelude & Nocturne
Sonata in C

Solo piano works by Myroslav Skoryk published in Ukraine and Russia

Blues: "Graiemo Jazz" (Playing Jazz), Works by Ukrainian Soviet Composers. Learning repertoire for Children's Music Schools. Kiev, Muzychna Ukraina, 1990 pp. 38-41

Blues: Myroslav Skoryk, Works for Piano; Kiev, Muzychna Ukraina, 1976 pp. 35-37

Boiko Song, Cycle: In Carpathian Mountains. Piano Pedagogical Repertoire; Course III –IV. Works of Ukrainian Soviet Composers: Issue #9. Kiev, Muzychna Ukraina, 1965 pp. 6-11

Burlesque: Kiev, Muzychna Ukraina, 1960

Burlesque: Kiev, Muzychna Ukraina, 1976 pp. 38-51

Folk Dance, Contemporary Piano Music for Children; Course IV. Learning repertoire for children's Music Schools. Kiev, Learning repertoire for children's Music Schools. Kiev, Muzychna Ukraina, 1970 pp. 30-32

Folk Dance, Cycle; From the Children's Album: Kiev, Muzychna Ukraina, 1970 pp. 4-6

Humorous Piece, Cycle; From the Children's Album: Playing Jazz; Works of Ukrainian Soviet Composers. Learning repertoire for children's Music Schools. Kiev, Muzychna Ukraina, 1970 pp. 13-15

In the Forest, Cycle; From the Children's Album: Myroslav Skoryk, Works for Piano; Kiev, Muzychna Ukraina, 1976 pp. 21-25

In the Forest, Cycle; From the Children's Album: Pieces by Ukrainian Composers. Moscow, Sovetskii Kompositor, 1971 pp. 65-68 compiled by B. Milich

In the Forest, Seventh Course in Piano, Part II; Kiev, Muzychna Ukraina, 1979 pp. 16-19

Kolomyika, Pedagogical Repertoire for Piano. Works of Ukrainian Soviet Composers: Issue #1. Kiev, Muzychna Ukraina, 1968 pp. 30-34

Kolomyika, Piano Works of Myroslav Skoryk. Kiev, Muzychna Ukraina, 1976 pp. 30-34

Kolomyika, Repertoire for Music Schools; Course I-II. Works of Ukrainian Soviet Composers: Issue #6. Kiev, Muzychna Ukraina, 1964 pp. 20-24

The Lyre Player, Cycle; From the Children's Album: Kiev, Muzychna Ukraina, 1970 pp. 9-12

The Lyre Player, Piano Works of Myroslav Skoryk. Kiev, Muzychna Ukraina, 1985 pp. 77-81

Partita No. 5, Kiev, Muzychna Ukraina, 1979

Piano Variations: Myroslav Skoryk, Works for Piano; Kiev, Muzychna Ukraina, 1976 pp. 3-15

Pop Song, Cycle; From the Children's Album: Kiev, Muzychna Ukraina, 1970 pp. 6-8

Pop Song, Works for Children by Ukrainian Composer's: Issue #1. Kiev, Muzychna Ukraina, 1976 pp. 105-107. Compiled by E. Rzhanov

Reiterating Tune, Playing Jazz; Works of Ukrainian Soviet Composers. Learning repertoire for children's Music Schools. Kiev, Muzychna Ukraina, 1990 pp. 34-38

Reiterating Tune, Stage and Jazz Pieces for Piano. Kiev, Muzychna Ukraina, 1987 pp.13-16

A Simple Melody, Contemporary Piano Music for Children; Course III. Kiev, Muzychna Ukraina, 1994 pp. 48-49 compiled by B. Milich

A Simple Melody, Works of Ukrainian Soviet Composers: Issue #1. Kiev, Muzychna Ukraina, 1976 pp. 88-89 compiled by E. Rzhanov

Singing in the Mountains, Piano Works of Myroslav Skoryk. Kiev, Muzychna Ukraina, 1976 pp. 25-29

**Twelve Preludes and Fugues for Piano,* Music book #1; Kiev, Muzychna Ukraina, 1989 (*Skoryk has only completed six of the twelve preludes and fugues to date).

Theoretical articles and essays by Myroslav Skoryk

Future of our Music (Maibutnie nashoi muzyky) Lecture of the Vice-President of the Ukrainian Composer's Union, 1971, No. 1, p. 8-9

Music Creation and Critique (Muzykalnoe tvorchestvo I kritika) *Public address on the fifth plenum of the board of administration of the Composers Union of the USSR.* Collection of articles and papers, Editor: G. Drubachevskaia, Moscow, Sovetskii Kompositor, 1974, p. 77-78

On Progressive and Dogmatic Innovations (O progressivnom I dogmaticheskom novatorstve) Sovetskaia Muzyka, 1971, No. 8, p. 17-23

Prokofiev and Schoenberg: Sovetskaia muzyka, 1962, No. 1

Sergei Prokofiev's Peculiarities of Modal Music (Osobennosti lada muzyki S. Prokofiev) Collection of articles compiled by K. Iuzhak, Moscow, Myzyka, 1972, p. 226-228

The Structural Aspects of Chords in 20th Century Music (Struktura I vyrazhalna pryroda akordyky v muzitsi XX stolittia) Myzychna Ukraina, Kiev, 1983

Word about a Composer (Slovo pro kompozytora – Ihor Sonevytsky) Myzychna Ukraina, Kiev, 1993, p. 5-6

Bibliography

Abraham, Gerald. *On Russian Music*. New York, Books for Libraries Press, 1939.

Adorno, Theodor. *Philosophy of New Music*. Minneapolis, University of Minnesota Press, 2006.

Albright, Daniel. *Modernism and Music*. Chicago, The University of Chicago Press, 2004.

Aldwell, Edward and Carl Schachter. *Harmony & Voice Leading*. 3rd ed. New York, Wadsworth Group, 2003.

Antokoletz, Elliott. *Twentieth-Century Music*. New Jersey, Prentice-Hall, 1992.

Ashby, Arved. *The Pleasure of Modernist Music*. Rochester, University of Rochester Press, 2004.

Austin, William. *Music in the 20th Century*. New York, W.W. Norton & Company, 1966.

Bakst, James. *A History of Russian-Soviet Music*. New York, Norton, 1966.

Bauer, Marion. *Twentieth Century Music*. New York, G.P. Putnam's Sons, 1933.

Berry, Wallace. *Form in Music*. New Jersey, Prentice-Hall, 1986.

———. *Structural Functions in Music*. New Jersey, Prentice-Hall, 1976.

Boyden, Matthew. *The Rough Guide to Opera*. 3rd ed. London, Rough Guides Ltd, 2002.

Broughton, Simon. *World Music Volume 1: Africa, Europe and the Middle East*. London, Rough Guides Ltd, 1999.

Burkholder, Peter J. and Donald Jay Grout and Claude V. Palisca. *A History of Western Music*. 7th ed. New York, W.W. Norton & Company, 2006.

Calvocoressi, Michael. *A Survey of Russian Music*. Westport, Greenwood Press, Publishers, 1974.

Caplin, William. *Classical Form*. New York, Oxford University Press, 1998.

Collaer, Paul. *A History of Modern Music*. Cleveland, The World Publishing Company, 1961.

Cone, Edward T. *Musical Form and Musical Performance*. New York, Norton, 1968.

Conquest, Robert. *The Harvest of Sorrow, Soviet Collectivization and the Terror-Famine*. Oxford, Oxford University Press, 1986.

Edmunds, Neil. *The Soviet Proletarian Music Movement*. Oxford, Peter Lang AG, European Academic Publishers, Bern 2000.

———. (editor) *Soviet Music and Society under Lenin and Stalin*. London, England. Routledge Curzon, 2004.

Forte, Allen. *The Structure of Atonal Music*. New Haven, Yale University Press, 1973.

Granowicz, Antoni. *Sergei Rachmaninoff*. New York, E.P Dutton and Company, Inc, 1946.

Greene, Douglass M. *Form in Tonal Music*. 2nd ed. New York: Holt, Rinehart and Winston, 1979.

Gridley, Mark. *Jazz Styles: History and Analysis*. 3rd ed. New Jersey, Prentice Hall, 1988.

Hepokoski, James and Warren Darcy. *Elements of Sonata Theory*. New York, Oxford University Press, Inc, 2006.

Ivashkin, Alexander. *Alfred Schnittke*. London, Phaidon Press Limited, 1996.

Keldysh, Y.V. Istoriia muzyki narodov SSSR [Music History of People-Republics of USSR, Vol. 5 Part I]. Moscow, Sovetski kompozitor, 1974.

Kostska, Stefan and Dorothy Payne. *Materials and Techniques of Twentieth-Century Music*. New Jersey, Prentice-Hall, 1999.

———. *Tonal Harmony*. 5th ed. New York, McGraw-Hill, 2004.

Krebs, Stanley. *Soviet Composers and the Development of Soviet Music*. New York, W.W. Norton & Company, 1970.

Kyianovska, Liubov. *Myroslav Skoryk: Tvorchyi portret kompozityora v dzerkali epokhy* [Creative Portrait of the Composer in a Mirror of Time]. Spolom, Lviv, 1998.

Lobanova, Marina. *Musical Style and Genre: History and Modernity*. Amsterdam, Harwood Academic Publishers, 2000.

Maes, Francis. *A History of Russian Music*. Los Angeles, University of California Press, 2002.

Metzer, David. *Quotation and Cultural meaning in Twentieth-Century Music*. Cambridge, Cambridge University Press, 2003.

Morgan, Robert. *Twentieth-Century Music*. New York, W.W. Norton & Company, 1991.

Nathan, M. Montagu. *A History of Russian Music*. London, William Reeves, 1918.

Olkhovsky, Andrey. *Music Under The Soviets*. London, Routledge & Kegan Paul LTD, 1955.

Perle, George. *Twelve-Tone Tonality*. Berkeley, University of California Press, 1977.

Puccini, Giacomo, *Madama Butterfly*. (Piano-Vocal Score), Mineola, Dover Publications, Inc., 2002.

Rahn, John. *Basic Atonal Theory*. New York, Schirmer Books, 1980.

Roberts, Peter Deane. *Modernism in Russian Piano Music, v. 1 & 2*. Bloomington, Indiana University Press, 1993.

Rosen, Charles. *The Classical Style: Haydn, Mozart, Beethoven*. New York, Norton, 1972.

Sabaneyeff, Leonid. *Modern Russian Composers*. New York, International Publishers, 1927.

Schwarz, Boris. *Music and Musical Life in Soviet Russia*. Bloomington, Indiana University Press, 1983.

Schwartz, Elliott. *Music Since 1945*. New York, Schirmer Books, 1993.
Seaman, Gerald. *History of Russian Music*. New York, Frederick A. Praeger, Publishers, 1967.
Shchyrytsia, Yuri Pavlovych. *Myroslav Skoryk*. Kiev, 1979.
Simms, Bryan. *Music of the Twentieth Century*. New York, Schirmer Books, 1996.
Sitsky, Larry. *Music of the Twentieth-Century Avant-Garde*. Westport, Greenwood Press, 2002.
———. *Music of the Repressed Russian Avant-Garde, 1900–1929*. Westport, Greenwood Press, 1994.
Starr, Frederick. *Red and Hot: The Fate of Jazz in the Soviet Union, 1917–1980*. Oxford, Oxford University Press, 1983.
Stelmakh, Bohdan. *Try ukrainski libretto* [Three Ukrainian libretti]. Spolom, Lviv, 2003.
Straus, Joseph. *Introduction to Post-Tonal Theory*. New Jersey, Prentice-Hall, 2005.
Stravinksy, Igor. *Poetics of Music*. Translated by A. Knodel and I. Dahl. Cambridge, Massachusetts, Harvard College, 1947.
Subtelny, Orest. *Ukraine; A History*. Toronto, University of Toronto Press, 1988.
Suchoff, Benjamin. *Bela Bartok Essays*. Lincoln, University of Nebraska Press, 1976.
Tymoshenko, O.S. Zbirnyk *naukovykh prots, prysviachenyi 60-richchiu vid dnia narodzhennia M.M Skoryka* [Scientific Herald, Ukrainian National Music Academy, Issue #10 Myroslav Skoryk; This issue dedicated to his 60th Birthday]. Kiev, 2000.
Uspenskaia, Sofia. *Soviet Literature on Music*—1960–1962. Moscow, All Union Publishers, 1967.
Volkov, Solomon. *Testimony, The Memoirs of Dmitri Shostakovich*. New York, Proscenium Publishers Inc, 1979.
Werth, Andrew. *Musical Uproar in Moscow*. Westport, Greenwood Press Publishers, 1949.
Wold, Milo. *An Introduction to Music and Art in the Western World*. Boston, McGraw Hill, 1996.
Yakubiak, Yarema. *Myroslav Skoryk: Zbirka statei* [Myroslav Skoryk: Collection of Articles]. Splolom, Lviv, 1999.

Index

Victor Radoslav Markiw

Dr. Victor R. Markiw is a Lecturer in Music in the Department of Visual and Performing Arts at the University of New Haven in West Haven, Connecticut. Dr. Markiw received his D.M.A. in Piano Performance, Music Theory and History from the University of Connecticut at Storrs.